What is Antizionism?
(... and is it Antisemitic?)

Henri Stellman

What is Antizionism?
(... and is it Antisemitic?)

A Short Handbook For Activists and Analysts

Aspekt Publishers

What is Antizionism? (... and is it Antisemitic?)
© Henri Stellman
© 2019 Uitgeverij ASPEKT / Aspekt Publishers
Amersfoortsestraat 27, 3769 AD Soesterberg, The Netherlands
info@uitgeverijaspekt.nl – http://www.uitgeverijaspekt.nl

Cover: Snegina Uzunova
Inside: Thomas Wunderink

ISBN: 9789463384179
NUR: 680

All rights reserved. No reproduction copy or transmission of this publication may be made without written permission.

Endorsements of "What is Antizionism?"

This is a thoughtful, moderate and important piece of work. It deserves wide exposure. Henri Stellman exposes, with forensic thoroughness, the nature of this racism disguised as a superficially plausible political ideology – "Antizionism." The evidence for the central thesis of the paper – that Antizionism and antisemitism are closely interlinked – is overwhelming. This is an insight with major implications for the discourse around the Arab-Israeli conflict. Readers will not fail to be impressed by the book's range, thoroughness, scholarliness and relevance to Israel's position in the world today.

David Stone
Emeritus Professor, University of Glasgow
Academic Director, StandWithUs UK

The issue of Antizionism including its origins, justifications, methods and proponents has long been a puzzle. The work of Dr. Henri Stellman is an enlightening compendium. Stellman shows that Israel and its citizens are being demonized, delegitimized and discriminated against. This study is a must-read and deserves serious scholarly attention.

Igal Ram
Founding Director, Firewall Israel
The Reut Institute

Table of Contents

Introduction — 11

A Note About the Author — 16

Part 1: The Foundation — 17

1. Definition of Antizionism — 19
2. Definition of Related Concepts — 20
3. The Motives of Antizionism — 24

Part 2: Is Antizionism Antisemitic? The Ideological Dimension — 25

Left Antizionism — 27

4. Karl Kaustky — 29
5. The Bund — 34
6. Eduard Bernstein — 38
7. Lenin — 39
8. Trotsky — 41
9. After 1917 — 43
10. Communist Parties in Non-Communist Countries — 45
11. After the Creation of Israel — 47
12. Contemporary Themes — 49

Conspiracy Antizionism — 51

13. Christian — 52
14. Nazi — 54
15. Neo-Nazi — 56
16. Deniers — 58

Christian Antizionism   60

17. "Deicide"   61
18. "Non-belief"   63
19. Other Christian Arguments   65

Jewish Antizionism   69

20. Emancipationism   70
21. Protest Rabbis   73
22. Protest Rabbis Followers   74
23. Breuer and Agudath Israel   76
24. Neturei Karta   78

Arab and Muslim Antizionism   80

25. Aims   81
26. Libels   83
27. Islam   87
28. "Colonialism/Imperialism"   90
29. "Apartheid" and Boycott, Disinvestment,   92
    Sanctions (BDS)

30. Coalescences of Antizionist Ideologies   94

Part 3: Is Antizionism Antisemitic? Other Dimensions   97

31. Violent Antizionism   98
32. The Antisemitic Aspect of Boycotts   100
33. Acknowledgement by Antizionists of Antisemitism   102
34. Zionism as a Code Word   104
35. Antizionism as Double-Standard   107
36. The Consequences of Antizionism   109
37. Fellow Antizionist Travellers   111
38. Separate Antisemitic and Antizionist Views in same   112
    individuals
39. Unintentional Antisemitism in Antizionism   114

Part 4: The Means of Antizionism   **117**

40. Violence   119
41. Cartoons   120
42. Boycott, Disinvestment and Sanction   123
43. Omissions of Facts and Misrepresentation   125
44. Falsifications   128
45. Decontextualization   129
46. Exaggerations   130
47. Double Standards   131
48. The Spheres   132

Part 5: Tools for Activists and Analysts   **133**

49. A short list of resources   135
50. Revision Questions   136
51. Training Exercise   147
52. Discussion Points   152

Index   154

Introduction

I have a particular hobby, some might call it a morbid hobby: I collect and analyse expressions of hostility to Zionism and the state of Israel in their various forms. It takes all sorts to make a world. Some people collect stamps, others engage in train spotting. I investigate what the enemies of Israel say.

This book is the culmination of forty years of fascination that I have had with the phenomenon of Antizionism. In the words of professor Alan Dershowitz, "no civilized nation in the history of the world, including totalitarian and authoritarian regimes, has ever been as repeatedly, unfairly, and hypocritically condemned and criticized by the international community as Israel has been over the years".[1]

My initial interest was in part a reaction to the fact that when I encountered the subject initially, I noticed that research into Antizionism had been neglected. Fast forward to the present-day, and I notice that even though various high-quality studies have been published, a long road still lies ahead towards a more comprehensive and systematic research into the subject as a global phenomenon. The body of research focuses on specific aspects of Antizionism but the general picture has been overlooked. In short, to use the well-known metaphor, there is a failure to see the forest for the trees.

With the danger that it represents to Israel and the Jewish people, I am mystified why the study of Antizionism remains in its infancy, why university chairs, institutes and learned journals dedicated to this phenomenon have not been created and why a study such as the one I have developed in this handbook has never been undertaken until now.

As my modest contribution to address this neglect, I embarked many summers ago, on a doctoral research on the ideologies of Antizionism, the first of its kind as far as I know. I gained my PhD at the London School of Economics and Political Science, under

---

1 Alan Dershowitz, *The Case for Israel*, New Jersey, 2003, p.222.

the supervision of the distinguished professor Elie Kedourie, with professor Robert Wistrich, a world authority on Antisemitism, acting as external examiner.

There were, and still are, three reasons why I chose this subject.

Firstly, anti-Zionism has, since 1967, progressed at a breath-taking speed.

As a result of the Six-Day war, Israel had its status of the weak and vulnerable party, overturned almost overnight. It became perceived as the 'Superdog' while the Arab counties and the Palestinians became the 'Underdogs'. This development was highlighted during the 1982 Lebanon War, and then subsequently by events linked to the West Bank, the Gaza Strip and Lebanon.

Whether it be at the United Nations, in the Middle East, on campuses, in the mass-media or elsewhere, Antizionism has become a very topical subject which I felt warranted serious investigation.

More specifically, and in view of the numerous discussions taking place on the subject, I was particularly interested to research the anti-Jewish dimension of Antizionism.

It is interesting to observe that Antizionists are very sensitive when charged with Antisemitism. This is so because of the stigma attached to Antisemitism. They are put in a difficult, uncomfortable and defensive position when accused of Antisemitism. They go into great length to deny that they are in any way Antisemitic, even going as far as to claim that accusations of Antisemitism levelled at them are used to silence them.[2] Clearly it bothers them.

Secondly, 'tacit indignant versum': my general abhorrence of Antizionism and a need to substantiate the reason for my indignation, were a further reason for my investigation.

---

2   David Hirsh, *Anti-Zionism and Antisemitism: Cosmopolitan Reflections,* The Yale Initiative for the Interdisciplinary Study of Antisemitism, Working Paper no.1, New Heaven, 2011. Other defence arguments are that Arabs cannot be Antisemitic as they are themselves Semites and that Jews that lived in Islamic countries have been well treated, see http://www.jewishvirtuallibrary.org/myths-and-facts-human-rights, checked on 16 April 2017. It is also argued in defence that there are Jews who are Antizionists, see Kenneth L. Marcus, *Is the Boycott, Divestment, and Sanctions Movement Anti-Semitic?* in *The Case Against Academic Boycotts of Israel,* ed. by Cary Nelson and Gabriel Noah Brahm, Chicago, 2015, p.254.

Finally, I had chosen to embark first on a doctoral research and now on this project in the hope that it would provide useful material in the fight against Antizionism. The better one knows ones' opponent, the better one is able to confront him. I am particularly concerned with the younger Jewish generation, on campuses and elsewhere, vulnerable, isolated, intimidated and harassed.

After completion of my doctorate, I worked for many years as an executive for various Israel-related organisations based in the United Kingdom, a well-known hub of anti-Israeli activism, and as such was able to watch Antizionist agitation at first hand. The nature of my responsibilities involved close encounters, amongst others, with the academic world, from university administrators and teaching staff to students, with the political elite, from the highest office right to grass-root activists, and with the media, from editors to specialised journalists. Travelling often up and down the country, I was able to get a fair gauge of a wide spectrum of society's attitude to Zionism and Israel.

Thus, I was able to combine academic research with practical experience.

My attitude to Antizionism is not purely negative. Whilst I take exception to those who aim to harm the State of Israel, and whilst I object to their argumentation, I must confess to having a certain fascination for the intellectual, analytical and organizational qualities to be found amongst some of the Antizionists.

My routine of recording and analyzing a vast record of vicious attacks on Zionism and Israel has enabled me to develop a certain immunity to those wild accusations. And yet this ideology has and still does often make my blood run cold sometimes.

It was clear that my approach had to be as simple, concise and reader-friendly as possible. I was interested in developing a handbook - as compact as possible - that could be used when and where required by circumstances. My aim was to analyse effectively a difficult and emotionally laden subject and help those encountering and willing to confront the debunkers of Zionism and Israel. In order to achieve that aim, I realised that it had to follow a number of rules:

use where possible easy language, provide a clear and attractive layout and classification, substantiate every assertion with quotes and were possible examples and provide carefully the several hundreds of sources used in this research.

I am also aware that Antizionism is active in various countries sometimes with regional variations. As I want this guide to be usable internationally, I have chosen to describe various Antizionist features across the world with particular attention to common features found in various countries.

I start my study by looking first at the foundation of Antizionism. Then I examine the important subject of the relationship between Antizionism and Antisemitism. Next, I focus on the means of Antizionism.

I have added at the end a section with a short list of resources for those who want to expand their interest, revision questions and discussion points. I have also added various quotes from Antizionists, without any comment, as a training exercise where I am inviting the readers to try to relate the quotes to the issues raised in this handbook.

In anticipation of the usual defence argument brought by those censuring Zionism and Israel, I state at the outset that I do not conflate opposition to Zionism and Israel and criticism of Israel's policies. One can legitimately oppose Israel's policies in the same way that one can legitimately oppose any other country's policies.

Some of the legitimate criticism can be found amongst Israelis and pro-Israelis including, increasingly, Jews of the Diaspora. Well-intentioned as they are, they have however magnified and emboldened the Antizionist campaign and re-enforced the self-righteousness of the enemies of the Jewish state.

This is a first attempt to tackle Antizionism in this particular way. I would welcome any suggestion to improve its content and presentation.

I owe thanks to numerous people who have helped me in one way or another in this long-lasting research. Friends, relatives, academics, work colleagues, typists, librarians, editors and many others too numerous to mention by name, have a hand in this project. I feel indebted to each and every one of them.

I dedicate this handbook to my late father Herbert Stellman and to my mother Anna, without whose help and encouragement I could never have undertaken this study; to my wife Eva, by way of thanking her for her steadfast support, invaluable comment and for putting up with the pressure of my research; last but not least, to my sons Natie and Ben, who, when I started the long journey that ended with the publication of this book, provided pleasant distractions from an all too serious study and who, since then, have graduated into fine young men who have also had their say on the subject.

H.S.

A note about the author

Originally from Belgium, Henri Stellman holds Bachelors and Masters degrees in International Politics and gained his doctorate on the Ideologies of Antizionism from the London School of Economics and Political Science. He holds further qualifications in finance, with certification in the field from the UK's Chartered Insurance Institute. Dr Stellman has lectured widely and has appeared on radio and television.

His various academic and non-academic articles have appeared in Parliamentary Affairs, Middle East Review, The Wiener Library Bulletin, The Times Higher Educational Supplement, The Guardian and many other publications. His work has been frequently cited in research literature and features on the recommended Reading Lists of universities. His expertise on various issues in international affairs has been regularly sought, and he has consulted to a variety of research institutes and media bodies. In 2016 he joined, as an analyst, the Firewall Israel unit of the Reut Institute.

Part 1

The Foundation

1.

Definition of Antizionism

Antizionism is the opposition to Zionism and/or the state of Israel.

- When it aims at bringing an end to the existence of the state of Israel, it can be called **Politicidal Antizionism.** [3]

- When it aims at *delegitimizing, dehumanizing, demonizing,* the state of Israel, it can be called **Anti-Israel Antizionism.**

    Delegitimatization is the attempt to take away the acceptance of Israel by the international community of nations.

    Dehumanisation is the attempt to deprive Israel and its inhabitants of positive human qualities.

    Demonization is the attempt to portray Israel as wicked.[4]

Each of the above two forms of Antizionism can stand alone or can appear in combination with the other.

Antizionism should not be conflated with criticism of Israel's policies. One can legitimately disapprove of Israel's policies in the same way that one can legitimately disapprove of any other country's policies.

3　Y. Harkabi, *Arab Attitudes to Israel,* Jerusalem, 1974, p.37.
4　For a discussion of these concepts, see E. Sprinzak, *Anti-Zionism: From Delegitimization to Dehumanization, Forum,* No.53, Fall 1984.

2.

Definition of Related Concepts

Antisemitism "Antisemitism is a certain perception of Jews, which may be expressed as hatred toward Jews. Rhetorical and physical manifestations of antisemitism are directed toward Jewish or non-Jewish individuals and/or their property, toward Jewish community institutions and religious facilities."

To guide IHRA [International Holocaust Remembrance Alliance] in its work, the following examples may serve as illustrations: Manifestations might include the targeting of the state of Israel, conceived as a Jewish collectivity. However, criticism of Israel similar to that levelled against any other country cannot be regarded as antisemitic. Antisemitism frequently charges Jews with conspiring to harm humanity, and it is often used to blame Jews for "why things go wrong." It is expressed in speech, writing, visual forms and action, and employs sinister stereotypes and negative character traits.

Contemporary examples of antisemitism in public life, the media, schools, the workplace, and in the religious sphere could, taking into account the overall context, include, but are not limited to:

- Calling for, aiding, or justifying the killing or harming of Jews in the name of a radical ideology or an extremist view of religion.
- Making mendacious, dehumanizing, demonizing, or stereotypical allegations about Jews as such or the power of Jews as collective — such as, especially but not exclusively, the myth about a world Jewish conspiracy or of Jews controlling the media, economy, government or other societal institutions.
- Accusing Jews as a people of being responsible for real or imagined wrongdoing committed by a single Jewish person or group, or even for acts committed by non-Jews.
- Denying the fact, scope, mechanisms (e.g. gas chambers) or intentionality of the genocide of the Jewish people at the hands of

National Socialist Germany and its supporters and accomplices during World War II (the Holocaust).
- Accusing the Jews as a people, or Israel as a state, of inventing or exaggerating the Holocaust.
- Accusing Jewish citizens of being more loyal to Israel, or to the alleged priorities of Jews worldwide, than to the interests of their own nations.
- Denying the Jewish people their right to self-determination, e.g., by claiming that the existence of a State of Israel is a racist endeavor.
- Applying double standards by requiring of it a behavior not expected or demanded of any other democratic nation.
- Using the symbols and images associated with classic antisemitism (e.g., claims of Jews killing Jesus or blood libel) to characterize Israel or Israelis.
- Drawing comparisons of contemporary Israeli policy to that of the Nazis.
- Holding Jews collectively responsible for actions of the state of Israel.

Antisemitic acts are criminal when they are so defined by law (for example, denial of the Holocaust or distribution of antisemitic materials in some countries).

Criminal acts are antisemitic when the targets of attacks, whether they are people or property – such as buildings, schools, places of worship and cemeteries – are selected because they are, or are perceived to be, Jewish or linked to Jews.

Antisemitic discrimination is the denial to Jews of opportunities or services available to others and is illegal in many countries".[5]

BDS is the initials for the "Boycott, Divestment and Sanction" campaign against Israel.

---

5   Resolution adopted by the *International Holocaust Remembrance Alliance*. https://www.holocaustremembrance.com/sites/default/files/press_release_document_antisemitism.pdf, Similar definitions have been adopted by other national and international institutions around the world.

The **Boycott** of Israel can be defined as a refusal to buy from, do business or collaborate with companies or organisations associated with the State of Israel as an expression of protest to the existence of the state or to its policies, or as a means to coerce Israel to alter its policies.

Divestment can be defined as the act of selling or disposing of an asset connected with Israel, with aims which are similar to the boycott.

Sanctions are a penalty or coercive measure against companies or organisations associated with Israel, also with aims similar to the boycott.

Differentiation To distinguish between the territory of the State of Israel and the territories occupied since 1967 by rejecting ties with Israel's developments beyond the 1967 line.[6]

Intersectionality "Proponents of intersectionality see a world of all-encompassing oppression, where racism, classism, sexism, homophobia and ableism constitute an intersecting system. All injustices are interconnected, even if occurring in unconnected geographic, cultural and political environments. This is the rationalization for building alliances among unrelated causes like LGBTQ rights, fossil fuel divestment, prison reform, racial discrimination and immigration. The anti-Israel BDS campaigns have successfully injected the Palestinians into this intersectional mix as victims of colonialist oppression by pro-Western Israel. The marriage of intersectionality with the Arab-Israeli conflict allows any victim group to make common cause with the Palestinians".[7]

Lawfare "A weapon designed to destroy the enemy by using, misusing, and abusing the legal system and the media in order to raise a public outcry against that enemy [i.e. Israel]". [8]

---

6   Herb Keinon, *Analysis: Differentiation clause will boost BDS, The Jerusalem Post*, 25 December 2016, http://www.jpost.com/Israel-News/Analysis-Differentiation-clause-will-boost-BDS-476430, checked on 4 January 2017.
7   Ziva Dahl, *The Observer*, 15 March 2016, http://observer.com/2016/03/intersectionality-and-the-bizarre-world-of-hating-israel/.
8   Tiefenbaum Susan, *Semiotic Definition of 'Lawfare'* (June17,2011) *Case*

Pink-washing is the allegation that Israel and its supporters are excessively emphasizing Israel's treatment and support for LGBT rights to cover-up its alleged "crimes".[9]

Western Reserve Journal Of International Law, Vol.43, 2011, Thomas Jefferson School of Law Research Paper No 1866448, available at SSRN: http://ssrn.com/abstract=1866448.

9   Based on Amir Ohana, Antizionists, talk to the Lid-East's gay community, *Jewish Chronicle*, 23 September 2016.

3.

The Motives of Antizionism

There is a rich tapestry of reasons why individuals choose their Antizionist stance. However, man's mind in unfathomable and often we do not know why some Antizionists have adopted their view because the motivation(s) is (are) not expressed or other motivations are expressed instead.

One can speculate what some of these motives might be and why they have not been expressed:

- Antisemitism
- In terms of geo-political and commercial considerations of realpolitik, it makes sense to align oneself to the view of the large, wealthy and influential Arab and Muslim world. Yet it would be unusual for anyone to acknowledge publicly such cynical motives.
- Psychological factors of which the Antizionists might not be aware are likely to play a role. Amongst those, one can suggest the phenomenon of "projection" in the Arab world, i.e. the propensity to attribute one's own negative qualities to the enemy. A guilt feeling for colonial rule in the Arab world and its excesses might well be a reason for the Antizionism of many Europeans.
- Antizionism is very likely to have been espoused by many people because it is fashionable, it is a trend to be followed and because it's perceived appeal as being politically correct.

Part 2

Is Antizionism Antisemitic?
The Ideological Dimension

Left Antizionism

- Left Antizionist ideology is the explanation and justification for this type of Antizionism. The historic interest of the ideologues of the Left has its origin in their concern for equality of men, for social well-being, for a better world. Their interest in the "Jewish Question" and their attempts to solve it, do not, therefore, come as a surprise.
- The prominent concern of the Left for the Jews is also to be explained by the prominent role played by Jews in the Socialist Movement. There are good reasons to believe that their attraction to Socialism lay in their conviction that the latter could offer a solution to the "Jewish Problem".
- However, there is a tradition of hostility to Judaism in Socialist ideology. From Proudhon to Kreitsky, including Marx, Engels, Kautsky, Stalin, Adler, Bauer and many more of the forefathers of Socialism, the Judeophobia of Socialist historic personalities is clearly evidenced.
- Bearing in mind the defence of the Jews taken by many supporters of the Left, and adding to this the decisive role played by Socialist Zionists in the establishment of the Jewish State and the subsequent support for Zionism and Israel adopted by many people on the Left around the world, one might have thought that the attitude towards Jewish self-determination would have been one of support. Yet the position that many people of the left have embraced has been one of opposition to the existence of the State of Israel and support of a campaign of delegitimization and dehumanisation of the State of Israel.
- It is interesting to note that Karl Marx never took a position on Zionism. Those who were going to oppose Zionism on the basis of the teachings of Marx have then either not specified his silence on the subject and therefore abuse his teachings, or deduce their Antizionism from Marx's teachings. A third possi-

bility would have been to speculate on what Marx might have said, had he written on Zionism.

- It could be speculated that had Marx written on Zionism, he would have rejected it. One could lean here on Marx's negative attitude to Judaism and the Jews. In *On the Jewish Question*, which he published in 1844 in the *Deutsch Franzosische Jahrbucher*, he called for the assimilation of Jews in their environment.[10] Marx being a Jew, this manifestation of Jew-hatred is to be seen as an act of self-hatred.
- What made things worse, is that he also uttered insulting remarks of the worst kind towards the Jews in his essay. Consider the following quote:

> "What is the profane basis of Judaism? Practical need, self-interest. What is the worldly cult of the Jew? Huckstering. What is his worldly god? Money. Very well: then in emancipating itself from huckstering and money, and thus from real and practical Judaism, our age would emancipate itself".[11]

- It has also been speculated that Marx's silence on Zionism is an indication of his rejection of it.[12]

---

10   Karl Marx, *On the Jewish Question, Karl Marx Early Writings*, T.B. Bottomore ed., London, 1963, pp.1-40.

11   ibid., p. 34, 'Practical', 'self-interest', 'Huckstering', 'Money' , 'huckstering', and 'money', are in italics in the text. The subject of Marx's attitude to Judaism has been profusely and diversely analysed. See, for example, Robert S. Wistrich, *Karl Marx and the Jewish Question, Soviet Jewish Affairs*, vol. 4, no. 1 , 1974, pp. 53-60; Robert Misrahi, *Marx et la Question Juive*, Paris, 1972; Annie Kriegel, *Les Juifs et le Monde Moderne*, Paris, 1977, pp.185-8; Nathan Weinstock, *Zionism: False Messiah*, London, 1979, pp. 266-70; Edmund Silberner, *Was Marx an Anti-Semite?*, *Historia Judaica*, vol. 11, no. 1, April 1949, pp. 3-52; Elisabeth de Fontenoy, *Les Figures juives de Marx*, Paris, 1973; Walid Sharif, *Soviet Marxism and Zionism*, *Journal of Palestine Studies*, vol. 6, no. 3, Spring 1977, pp. 78-81.

12   For the formulation of this idea, see Misrahi, ibid, pp.32-3. On the other hand, it has also been speculated that had Marx written on this, he would have embraced it; For the formulation of this idea, see Norman Levine, *Karl Marx and the Arab-Israeli Conflict, Judaism*, vol.19, no.2, Spring 1970, pp. 145-6.

4.

Karl Kaustky

- Karl Kautsky, the chief theoretician of the international labour movement, the Second International, and the leading theoretician of the German Social Democracy at the turn of the century, was "for many years the most respected interpreter of Marxist doctrine for West and East European Socialists alike".[13] Hence the importance of his writings, coupled with the fact that his views on Zionism, in those times "were the most consistent and systematic in their exposition of the Marxist arguments against Zionism".[14]
- According to another observer, in those times Kautsky "came closest to applying the Marxist method of historical materialism in a coherent fashion to the Jewish national problem".[15] The same observers have also highlighted the importance of Kaustky because his position contained, in embryonic form, the seeds of latter day Communist, Trotskyist and New Left critiques of Zionism.[16]
- Kautsky's Antizionism was the necessarily corollary of his views on how to solve the Jewish problem. For him, the Jews were not to be considered a nation as they were lacking a common territory and a common language; he saw them as a caste, like castes of India, sharing common features amongst themselves.[17] Kautsky was deeply convinced of their irreversible self-dissolution, their assimilation

---

13 Walter Laqueur, *A History of Zionism*, New York, 1972. p.417.
14 Ibid. p. 420.
15 Robert S. Wistrich, *German Social Democracy and the Problem of Jewish Nationalism, Year Book of the Leo Baeck Institute*, vol. 21, 1976, p.109.
16 Laqueur, op.cit, p.417; Wistrich, ibid.
17 Karl Kautsky, *Nationalitat und Internationalitat, Die Neue Zeit*, supplement, no.1, 18 January 1908, p.7. Kautsky was the editor of this leading review of German National Democracy. Wistrich, ibid. For the Antizionism of lesser known contributors to the journal, see Wistrich, ibid., pp.119-23.

in their environment with the coming of the new Socialist order.[18]
- He did not see this as a tragedy comparable to extinction or forced assimilation of other people, but as a progressive step.[19] It would end the misery, the Antisemitism to which they are subjected.[20] The Jews have the qualities most required for the progress of humanity; they have produced people like Spinoza, Heine, Lassalle, and Marx.[21]

> "Judaism has become a reactionary factor. It is like a weight of lead attached to the feet of the Jews who eagerly seek to progress, one of the last remnants of the feudal Middle Ages, a social ghetto still maintaining its existence in the consciousness, after the tangible, physical ghetto has disappeared. We cannot say we have completely emerged from the Middle Ages as long as Judaism still exists among us. The sooner it disappears, the better it will be not only for society, but also for the Jews themselves".[22]

- The disappearance of the Jews was not seen as a decline but as an ascent.

> "Ahasverus, the Wandering Jew, will at last have found a haven of rest. He will continue to live in the memory of man as man's greatest sufferer, as he who has been dealt with most severely by mankind, to whom he has given most".[23]

- Zionism was seen as a reaction to the inevitability of Jewish disappearance and therefore as reactionary. It wanted to maintain Jewish particularity and solidarity, stimulating the separation of

---

18   Karl Kautsky, *Are the Jews a Race?*, London, 1926, pp. 240-7. This is in fact a translation of the second edition of the book *Rasse und Judentum*, Stuttgart, 1921, the first edition having appeared in *Die Neue Zeit*, supplement, no. 20, 30 October 1914, pp. 1-94.
19   Kautsky, *Are the Jews a Race?*, ibid., p. 126.
20   ibid., p.244.
21   ibid., p.245.
22   ibid., p.246.
23   ibid., p.247.

Jew from non-Jew and by doing so and by considering Jewish presence in the Diaspora as temporary, Zionism was in fact espousing the thesis of the Antisemites and thus weakening the revolutionary movement.

> "The Zionist Movement could only reinforce the anti-Semitic feelings of the popular masses, in that it increases the segregation of the Jews from the rest of the population and brands them even more than before, as an alien nation, which, according to its outlook, has nothing to expect on the Russian soil".[24]

- Kautsky also claimed that Zionism, by advocating a Jewish State for the preservation of the Jewish race, was in fact adopting an anti-Judaism with racist character. "Palestine as world ghetto for the separation of the Jewish race from the other races, this has become the end of Zionism", he wrote in the 1914 edition of his *Rasse und Judentum*.[25]
- What was even worse for him was the actual collaboration of Zionists with Antisemitic forces. He wrote that "there have even been Zionists who expected much gracious assistance in the realisation of their objects from the head of the Orthodox Russian nation, from the fountainhead of anti-Semitism all over the world, from the Czar of Russia". [26] Kautsky must undoubtedly have been referring to the encounter, in August 1903, in Russia, between Herzl and Russian dignitaries, notably Plehve, the Russian Minister of Interior. As a result of their meeting, Plehve promised not to hinder Zionism as long as it encouraged emigration of Jews from Russia and did not engage in any political activity. He furthermore promised that the Russian government would intervene on behalf of Zionism with the Ottoman Sultan.[27]

---

24 Karl Kautsky, *Das Massaker von Kischineff und die Judenfrage, Die Neue Zeit*, vol. 2, no. 36, 1902-1903, p. 308.
25 Kaustky, *Rasse und Judentum,* 1914, op. cit., p. 82.
26 Kautsky, *Are the Jews a Race?,* op. cit., p. 183.
27 *The Complete Diaries of Theodor Herzl,* R. Patai ed., London, vol. 4, 1960,

- Kautsky also analysed Zionism within the Palestinian context. He stressed that there were no other vacant areas in the world where Jewish self-determination could be implemented.[28] He considered that without agriculture, Zion could not possibly be built and he thought that the Jews could not be turned from the city-dwellers they had been for so long into farmers.[29]
- What is more, in Palestine, transport was non-existent.[30] The soil was infertile[31], and the prospect of attracting foreign investors was small.[32] A large Jewish immigration, thus, would not be supported[33], and Jewish immigration anyway had not been exactly forthcoming up till that time.[34] The likelihood of the Zionist experience succeeding was small.
- Kautsky's strong opposition to British colonialism in Palestine, which he uttered in 1921, supplemented his criticism of Zionism, which he saw as an instrument of British imperialism, a view so forcefully defended up till today by Leftist Antizionist Jews. This unholy organic alliance, for him, meant that "Jewish colonisation in Palestine must collapse as soon as the Anglo-French hegemony over Asia Minor (including Egypt) collapses, and this is merely a question of time, perhaps of the very near future".[35]
- He predicted a clash between the Jewish settlers and the local Arab population and he was firmly convinced of the ultimate

---

pp. 1520-43.
28 Kautsky, *Are the Jews a Race?*, op. cit., ibid., p. 184.
29 ibid., pp. 185-6.
30 ibid., p. 187.
31 ibid.
32 ibid.
33 ibid., p. 188.
34 ibid.
35 ibid., p. 211. This and the following is taken from a chapter which Kautsky added in the second edition of his book *Rasse und Judentum*, published in 1921, op. cit., and the 1926 English translation, op.cit. It is chapter 10, pp. 193-215 of the English edition – to which we refer here – and is entitled *Zionism after the War*.

victory of the Arabs.[36] He was very apprehensive that this victory would lead to a tragic end, for the Jewish settlers were despised by the Arabs, defenceless and least capable of escaping.[37] He hoped that the Zionist settlement would proceed very slowly so as to limit the number of casualties.[38]

- Kautsky was honest to recognize and be impressed by the early and yet limited success of Zionism: "Anyone who has doubted the possibility of the Jewish people's showing energy, resolution and intelligence in· this crisis, must surely have changed his mind by reason of the work of Zionist reconstruction in Palestine".[39] However, he was of the opinion that the enthusiasm would not persist.[40]

- In a nutshell, one can say that if Kautsky opposed Zionism, at the same time his gloomy forecast for the future of the movement made him consider as superfluous the need for an active opposition.

---

36 ibid., pp. 211-2.
37 ibid., p. 212.
38 ibid., pp. 212-3.
39 ibid., p. 202.
40 Ibid., pp. 204-5.

5.

The Bund

- In October 1887, in Vilna, Jews from five cities in the Pale of Settlement decided to create a Jewish Socialist party[41] which subsequently took the name of Algemeyner Yidisher Arbeter Bund in Lite, Poyln un Rusland, i.e. the General Jewish Workers' Union in Lithuania, Poland and Russia, commonly known as the Bund.[42] The attitude of the Bund towards Zionism was one of fierce opposition.
- The Bundists were strong defenders of Jewish values and identity and engaged in efforts of education to preserve these idiosyncrasies. What is more, they developed an aggressive theory of Autonomism, arguing for their right to control their language, custom, way of life and culture as they saw fit.
- Their Antizionism had two lines of argument: they argued that Zionism was against Socialism but they were also against Zionism because of the situation in Palestine.
- *Di Arbeter Shtime*, the official organ of the Central Committee of the Bund[43], wrote that the bourgeois Zionists were unable to deal with the economic condition of the Jewish proletariat and worse even, that they were simply indifferent to it.[44] The Zionist stand which considered the Jews as alien in the Diaspora and refused any confrontation with the established authority was severely criticised. They said, it denies the possibility of a socialist

---

41 *Encyclopaedia Judaica*, vol. 4, Jerusalem, 1971, p. 1499.
42 Ibid., p. 1497. The original name did not include Lithuania which was eventually added. Henry J. Tobias, *The Jewish Bund in Russia*, Stanford, 1972, pp. 68, 165.
43 Tobias, op.cit., p.47.
44 *Der Fierter Tsionistishen Kongress, Die Arbeter Shtime*, no. 21, January 1901, pp. 4-7, in ibid., p. 128.

struggle in Russia.[45] It was also argued that it was historically wrong to say that Jews were strangers in Russia:

> "[O]ur ancestors came as peaceful dwellers, and in the course of a thousand years, together with the surrounding population, aided ·in the cultural development of the land, watering it with sweat, soaking it with their blood, and covering it with their bones… this land is our home".[46]

- It was also argued that the policy of living quietly in Russia would lead to an increasingly slavish Jewish population.[47] Zionism was accused of paying lip-service to the anti-Semitic anti-Socialist Tsarist government; the relative tolerance by the Russian government of Zionism and the willingness of Zionists to accept a certain collaboration in order to further their aim, was seen by Bundists with deep suspicion. The permission given in 1899 to the Zionist-oriented journal *Der Jud* to be sent from Cracow to Russia[48] and later the permission given in 1903 for the publication in Russia of another Zionist journal *Der Fraind*[49], was seen as an attempt to cloud class consciousness [50], to draw workers away from the Bund.[51]
- The second line of argument developed by the Bund referred to the situation in Palestine. It was affirmed that Zionism dispossessed the native population [52]; additionally that it wants to create a Class-state in Palestine and by so doing "conceal the

---

45 *Di Poale Zion…, Die Arbeter Shtime*, no. 37, June 1904, pp. 5-6, in ibid., p.253.
46 *Der "Bund" un di onfirer…, Der Bund*, no. 1, January 1904, p. 3, in ibid.
47 *Poale Zion…, Die Arbeter Shtime*, no. 33, May 1903, p. 5, in ibid., p. 249.
48 *Arkady: Zamlbukh tsum andenk fur Arkady Kremer*, New York, 1942, p. 328, in ibid., p.252; date mentioned on p.251.
49 Saul Ginzburg, *Amolike Peterburg: Forshungen un zikhroinos vegn yidishn lebn in der rezidents-shtot fun tsarishn Rusland*, New York, 1944, pp. 186-190, in ibid.
50 *Der Fraind, Die Arbeter Shtime*, no. 33, May 1903, pp. 9-11, in ibid., p.252.
51 *Arkady: Zamlbukh*, op.cit., p. 238, in ibid.
52 David Balakan, *Die Socialdemokratie und das judische Proletariat*, Czernowitz, 1905, in John Bunzl, *Klassenkampf in der Diaspora*, Vienna, 1975, p. 112.

class confrontation in the name of general national interests".[53] Zionist capital would exploit the cheap Arab labour force.[54] Are the Zionist-Socialists considering the implementation of a discriminatory law again the immigration of non-Jewish workers, it was asked.[55] But, it was claimed, the dispossessed would not remain idle.[56]

- Though well known for its role during the pre-1917 Russian Revolution, the Bund is less widely known for its continuous activity up till today. It played a very important role in Poland until 1948.[57] In the United States, the Bund was very active.[58] Moreover, an International of the Bund was created and held several conferences.[59] Opposition to Zionism and the State of Israel was often expressed.
- Immediately after the Revolution, Zionist 'rapprochement' with Great Britain, epitomized in the just issued Balfour Declaration, attracted the Bund's criticism. Britain was considered an imperialist power whose aim, by issuing the Declaration, was to convince the Russian Jews to urge their government to continue their involvement in the war; it was naive, they said, to trust British imperialists to give a homeland.[60]
- Vladimir Medem, an important figure of Russian Bundism, was of the opinion that Zionists were betraying the Diaspora and meddling unjustifiably in what they had abandoned.

> "Journey preparations, travel-fever! Pack your belongings! Turn your back on our life, on our struggle, on our joys and sorrows. You have decided to desert the Galuth! Well, leave it in peace. Don't interfere in our affairs, don't show your generosity by throwing alms ... [to us] ... from the window

---

53   Balakan, ibid., in ibid., p.111.
54   A. L., *Der Poale-Zionismus, Die Neue Zeit*, vol. 1.2., no. 25, 1905-1906, p.809.
55   Ibid.
56   Balakan, op.cit., p. 36, in Bunzl, op.cit., p. 113.
57   *Encyclopaedia Judaica*, op.cit., pp. 1503-5.
58   Ibid., p. 1506.
59   Ibid.
60   *Folkstseitung*, 22 November 1917, in Gitelman, op.cit., p. 76.

of your rail carriage - and, please, don't talk about defending our rights here".[61]

- For Emanuel Scherer, a leader of the Bund in the United States, the State of Israel would only be an ephemeral phenomenon in view of the inevitability of the Arab ascendency.[62] Dwelling on nationalism which he calls "chauvinistic", Scherer claims that it is senseless in a physically weak people and in general wicked because it is "a dreadful poison which sickens the relations between individuals and between peoples".[63] He points to the "limited absorptive capacity of Palestine".[64] He is dismayed by Zionist propaganda making us believe that there always will be anti-Semitism, leading to a permanent distrust of all the Gentiles.[65] He also staunchly believes in the prevention of a repetition of such a catastrophe as the Holocaust, and in a betterment of the world in which the Jews may be able to contribute.[66]
- Liebmann Hersh, another Bundist, notes that the eighty years of existence during which the Jewish People has lived united in an independent state - the kingdoms of Solomon and David - was infinitesimal in relation to the Jewish history: about two percent of that history, according to the skilful arithmetic of this writer.[67] He furthermore asserts that the most creative forces of Jewish antiquity developed at the time of the decadence of the State of Judah and later in Babylonian exile of the Jews and that Jewish spiritual leaders, at crucial moments of Jewish history, opposed a Jewish state.[68]

---

61 Howard M. Schahar, *The Course of Modern Jewish History*, London, 1958, p. 294. Sachar gives the date of this event as 1918; [to us] is added by Sachar.
62 Emanuel Scherer, *The Bund*, in *Struggle for Tomorrow, Modern political ideologies of the Jewish people*, B.J. Vlavianos and F. Gross eds., New York, 1954, p. 172.
63 Ibid., p. 192.
64 Ibid., p. 172.
65 Ibid., p. 152.
66 Ibid., p. 153.
67 L. Hersch, *The Independent State in Jewish History*, Unser Tsait, nos. 4-5, 1949, in ibid., p.166.
68 Ibid

6.

Eduard Bernstein

- Eduard Bernstein who was also of Jewish descent, repeatedly changed his views on Judaism. He fluctuated between his support for the Jews' affirmation of their identity and subscribing to the stand that assimilation was a necessity.[69]
- Although subsequently changing his views later on,[70] Bernstein was very critical towards Jewish national self-determination. Comparing Zionism with an epidemic, he wrote that he was convinced that the fate of this Zionist "intoxication" would be like that of an epidemic: it will vanish. Its disappearance, according to Bernstein, would not be immediate since it was part of a "nationalistic reaction" which had inundated "world bourgeoisie" and was also trying to penetrate world socialism.[71]

---

69 Robert S. Wistrich, *Revolutionary Jews from Marx to Trotsky*, London, 1976, pp. 60-75; Eduard Bernstein, *Das Schlagwort und der Anti-semitismus*, Die Neue Zeit, vol. 2, no. 35, 1892-1893, pp. 236-7; Eduard Bernstein, *Die Aufgaben der Juden im Weltkriege*, Berlin, 1917.

70 Bernstein, *Die Augaben*, ibid., p.32. Wistrich, *Revolutionary Jews*, pp. 70,71,74,75.

71 Eduard Bernstein, *Der Schulstreit in Palastina*, Die Zeit, vol.2., no. 20, issued on 13 February 1914, pp. 744-5, 752.

7.

Lenin

- Lenin saw the Jews divided into two very different categories: those living in Russia and Galicia and those living in Western countries. Referring to the first group, Lenin wrote that they live in Galicia and Russia, backward and semi barbarous countries, where the Jews are forcibly kept in the status of a caste.[72]
- What did Lenin understand by this categorisation of Jews as a "caste"? This definition was, as we saw, first used by Kautsky. It has been suggested that Lenin characterisation stemmed first from the propensity of Jews to maintain their distance from their environment and their ritual requirement of purity imposed by the religious laws in respect of acts of daily life.[73]
- Secondly it stemmed from the Jewish religion itself and its traditions, from the Jews' isolation from the centres of social articulation and their confinement to professional specialisation, in particular those professions morally despised and condemned but nevertheless essential for the good working of society. It is therefore not surprising that Lenin did not consider the Jews as a class or a nation, for the latter categories were based on completely different criteria.[74]
- Lenin argued his case by stressing that the Jews had no territory nor a language and that a nation without territory and language was unthinkable.[75] He advocated the assimilation of Jews in their environment, arguing that there was no other solution for

---

72 Lenin, *Critical Remarks on the National Question, Collected Works*, vol. 20, Moscow, 1964, p.26.
73 Annie Kriegel, *Les Juifs et le Monde Moderne*, Paris, 1977, p.194.
74 Ibid.
75 Lenin, *The Position of the Bund in the Party, Collected Works*, vol. 7, Moscow, 1961, p.99.

the Jews than their blending into the general mass of the population.⁷⁶ He wanted the Jews of the Pale of Settlement to follow the example set by their brethren in the Western countries:

> "[T]here the Jews do not live as a segregated caste. There the great world-progressive features of Jewish culture stand clearly revealed: its internationalism, its identification with the advanced movement of the epoch…the best Jews, those who are celebrated in world history, and have given the world foremost leaders of democracy and socialism, have never clamoured against assimilation".⁷⁷

- According to Lenin, anyone who is resisting this trend, like the Bundists or the Zionists "contemplates the rear aspect of Jewry with reverential awe". He is an enemy of the proletariat, a supporter of all that is outmoded and connected with caste among the Jewish people; he is an accomplice of the rabbis and the bourgeoisie, "a Jewish reactionary philistine, who want to turn back the wheel of history"⁷⁸… and foster the spirit of the ghetto.⁷⁹
- Observers have noted that subsequently Lenin changed his position regarding the Jews and came to accept them as a nationality. Yet this did not affect his extreme Antizionism.⁸⁰

---

76 Ibid. p.101.
77 Lenin, *Critical Remarks,* op.cit., pp.26 and 29.
78 Ibid., p.26-29.
79 Lenin, *The Position,* op.cit., p.101.
80 Norman Levine, *Lenin on Jewish Nationalism, The Wiener Library Bulletin,* vol. 33, nos. 51-52 (new series), 1980, pp.46-51.

8.

Trotsky

- Trotsky, another Jewish revolutionary who played a leading role in the Communist Movement, also combined Antizionism with Antisemitism. He believed

  > "that to make the Jews a special topic of discussion or to engage in a particularistic struggle against anti-Semitism was superfluous. The advent of the classless, socialist society would automatically 'solve' the problem".[81]

- Trostky's Antizionism was motivated by a deep animosity towards the founder of modern Zionism, Theodor Herzl, calling him a "shameless adventurist, a repulsive figure" whom he accused of "devilish perfidy, impudence and diplomatic chicanery and deceit".[82]
- Looking at the situation in Palestine, he was of the opinion that the conflict between Jews and Arabs could not be resolved within the framework of "rotting capitalism and under the control of British imperialism".[83] The attempts to solve the Jewish question through the migration of Jews to Palestine was a "tragic mockery of the Jewish people".[84]
- Interested in winning the sympathies of the Arabs who are more numerous than the Jews, the British government, according to Trotsky, had sharply altered its policy towards the Jews and had actually renounced its promise to help them found their own

---

81   Robert S Wistrich, *Jewish Chronicle,* 15 February 1980.
82   Joseph Nedava, *Trotsky and the Jews,* Philadelphia, 1972, p.197.
83   Leon Trotsky, interview of 18 January 1937, *Fourth International,* December 1945, *On the Jewish Question, New York, 1970,* p.20.
84   The Trotsky Archives, in Nedava, op.cit., p.209.

home in a foreign land. The future could well transform the country into a bloody trap for several hundred thousand Jews.[85]
- Trostky was not to see his promised land of World Socialism. He was to succumb to the terrible wound inflicted by an ice-pick in the hand of one of Stalin's hatchet man.[86]

---

85 Ibid.
86 Wistrich, Revolutionary Jews, op.cit., p.207.

9.

After 1917

- After the Russian revolution and the accession of the Bolsheviks to power in 1917, Left Antizionism now benefitted from a powerful state apparatus to implement its ideology.
- Regarding the international scene, the new rulers saw themselves as radically opposed and threatened by capitalist-imperialist powers. Britain's conquests in the Middle East and its support for a Jewish homeland, as expressed through the Balfour Declaration, were considered with the utmost aversion.[87]
- On the domestic level in Russia, Zionism was seen as "a movement that includes almost all the Jewish intelligentsia" and when successful

    > "it will immediately take from us large numbers of workers such as engineers, doctors, pharmacists, architects, and other specialists, whom we badly need in order to build up our national economy and whom we are obliged to honour because of our inferiority.[88] Zionist propaganda causes real damage… as it always delayed the association of the Jewish masses with the revolutionary movement".[89]

---

87 *Die Idishe Komisariatn un di Idishe Kommunistische Sektsiyes: Protokoln. Rezolutsiyes, un Dokumentn,* S. Agursky ed., Minsk, 1928, p. 228 in Guido G. Goldman, *Zionism under Soviet Rule (1917-1928),* New York, 1960, p.21; *Jewish Chronicle,* 1 March 1918.

88 Khozer Sodi me-et Ve. Ts. Ka. Al Ha-milkamah Betnuah Ha-tsionit, Iuli 1920, in Arieh Lieb Tsentsiper, Esser Sch'not R'difot, Tel Aviv, 1930, p.270, in Ran Marom, The Bolsheviks and the Balfour Declaration 1917-1920, The Left Against Zion, R.S. Wistrich ed., London, 1979, p. 23.

89 *Tazkir Me-et Ha-vaad ha-rashi shel HA-brit Ha-yehudit 'Komfarband' Be-Ukrainah el Hakomisarion Le-inianei Pnim shel Ukrainah, 4 Iuli 1919,* in Arieh Lieb Tsentiper, op.cit, p.262.

- The Zionists were accused of bringing out the "ugliness of Jewish life".[90] Whereas the bad conditions in pre-revolutionary Russia made Jews understandably choose Zionism, it was asserted, the advent of Socialism was making things good for them: it was opening the gates to civil progress, allowing the Jews to become partners in ruling the country and actively participating in its future.[91] Why then should they aspire for a Jewish State, let alone in a distant and isolated country, it was asked.[92]
- After the Second World War, the Soviet Union resumed its attacks on Zionism. It was described as a reactionary nationalist political trend emerging and becoming widespread in a period when Antisemitic persecution and repression were visited upon the Jewish popular masses. It was claimed that Zionists look upon Antisemitism as inevitable and eternal. Zionism was criticised for supporting class co-operation with the Jewish bourgeoisie and distracting the toiling Jews from struggling in common with the toilers of other nationalities. The mantra of the link of Zionism with imperialism was also prominent.[93]

---

90   Z. Greenberg, *Die Zionisten oif der Idisher Gas,* Petrograd, 1918, p.19, in Goldman, op.cit., p.38.
91   Yoseph Barzilai, *Sichoth Im Schimon Dimanshtein, Heavar,* vol. 15, May 1968, p.231.
92   Ibid.
93   Entry on Zionism in *Bolshaya Sovetskaya* encyclopaedia, vol. 51, 1945, in Lukas Hitsczowicsz, *Soviet Perceptions of Zionism, Soviet Jewish Affairs,* vol. 9, no.1/1, 1079, p.55.

10.

Communist Parties in Non-Communist countries

- Opposition to Zionism has also been expressed by diverse Communist parties in non-Communist countries. For example, the Palestine Communist Party, made up of Jews and Arabs, combined traditional themes with new ones. Among the old themes were the opposition to the imperialist power, Great Britain.[94] More original were the attacks on the Palestinian and Arab countries' leadership for their disastrous policies towards Zionism and Britain.[95] Equally novel were the expressions of solidarity with the local peasants[96], the assault of the Arab feudal landlords who sold their lands to the Zionists, thereby depriving the peasants of their earnings[97], and the appeal to Jewish workers to espouse the cause of their fellow Arab workers against the Zionists.[98]
- Very similar was the Antizionism of the American Communist Party. A permutation with local flavour was however noticeable.

---

94   'The Revolt in Palestine', Communique of the Central Committee of the Palestine Communist Party, *Inprecor,* nos. 54 and 56, 1929, in Musa Budeiri, *The Palestine Communist Party 1919-1948,* London 1979, p.30.

95   Interview with Nimr Odeh of the Palestinian Commnist Party, Beirut, 10 March 1974, op.cit., p.96. Leaflet of the Central Committee of the Palestine Communist Party, *Falastin,* 14 September 1936, in ibid.

96   'To the Masses of Oppressed Peasants: Life or Death,' Arabic Leaflet of the Central Committee of the Palestine Communist Party, January 1930, in ibid., p.52; 'Remember Peasant', unsigned Arabic leaflet adorned with the Hammer and Sickle, 1932, in ibid.

97   'The Tasks of the Palestine Communist Party in the Countryside', Resolutions of the Seventh Congress of the Palestine Communist Party, 1930, pp. 170,174, in ibid., p.71.

98   'Instruction of Palestine Communist Party Secretariat to the members', Circular Letter no.3, May 1932, in ibid., p.55.

British imperialism was attacked[99], but so was the United States' role in the Zionist-capitalist framework[100]. On one hand, there were the local Arabs, in the glorious struggle for their own country[101], together with the deceived Jewish masses[102], on the other hand, there were the imperialist-capitalist powers and the Zionists, guilty of segregation[103], cowardice[104] and fascism.[105]

---

99   *Freiheit,* 27 July 1922, in Stuart Eugene Knee, *Vision and Judgment: The American Critics of the Zionist Movement, 1917-1941,* Ann Arbor, 1974, p.293.
100 *Freiheit,* 29 October 1930, in ibid., p.297; *The Revolutionary Age,* 22 November 1930, in ibid.
101 Statement by Melech Epstein at a Communist picnic in Cleveland, *The Daily Worker,* 7 September 1929, in ibid., p.295.
102 *The Daily Worker,* 3 September 1929, in ibid.
103 *The Workers Age,* 30 May 1936, in ibid., p.301.
104 *Freiheit,* 31 August 1929, in ibid., p.294.
105 *The Revolutionary Age,* 11 July 1931, in ibid., p.298.

11.

After the Independence of Israel

- Whilst supporting Israel aspirations for Jewish statehood, the Soviet Union has called for a return to the 1947 Partition's borders, a call which has been laced with the traditional communist ideology: Israel's bourgeois leaders branded as tools of Anglo-American imperialism and the claim of exploitation of the Israeli working class by their bourgeois government.[106]
- An unparalleled campaign of vilification of Zionism, where exorbitant allegations and crude languages were prominent, was inaugurated in 1963 with the publication by the Ukrainian Academy of Science of Trofim Kichkos' *Judaism without Embellishment*. The book identified Judaism with the greed and usury of Jewish bankers, with Zionism, Israel and Western capitalism in a universal dark conspiracy.[107]
- Israel's victory over the Arabs who were supported by the Soviets, in the 1967 Six-Day war, brought about a campaign of vicious assault. According to the Ukrainian magazine *Peretz* of October 1967,

    "German Zionist bankers have opened generously their safe to Hitler…Threblinka's gas chambers were built with money of the 'Aryan' Zionists…Italian Zionists have helped Mussolini to take power…Now, even the most orthodox Zionists would be incapable of denying that all the major

---

106 revolutionarydemocracy.org/rdv12n2/ehrenburg.htm, checked on 27 March 2017.
107 http://www.ajcarchives.org/AJC_DATA/Files/668.PDF, checked on 27 March 2017.

crimes against humanity were not committed with the Zionists' participation".[108]

- According to *International Affairs,* Israel policy in the occupied Arab territories

    "[i]nvoluntarily brings to mind Nazi practices during the Second World War. There is the same immediate appointment of Gauleiters for the newly-occupied areas; the ruthless treatment of POW's and the native population; the terrorism and eviction of the population from their old homeland; the plunder and 'development' of occupied territories…all…sickeningly reminiscent of Hitler's 'new order in Europe' ".[109]

- All this was a very far cry from the Antizionist critique of the forefathers of Left Antizionism.

---

108 *Les Juifs en Europe de l'Est,* no. 24, p.28, in Leon Poliakov, *De L'Antisionisme a L'Antisemitisme,* Paris, 1969, p.127.
109 L. Sedin, *The Arab people's Just Cause, International Affairs,* no.8, 1967, p.26. in Baruch A. Hazan, *Soviet Propaganda – A case Study of the Middle East Conflict,* Jerusalem, 1976, p.161.

12.

Contemporary Themes

- An analysis of Left Antizionism would be incomplete without mentioning those groups that go under the banner of the illustrious forefathers of the ideology of the Left: Marxists, Leninists, Trotskyists, Stalinists, Maoists and others, whose marginality, extremism of views and success among young people, specifically on campus, are well known.
- The chief Trotskyist ideologist on Zionism[110], was Abraham Leon, a Belgian Jew who considered that Zionism was a result of Antisemitism.[111] Zionism, in his eyes, was helped by the Jewish bourgeoisie who wanted those Jews who immigrated to Western countries to instead "go as far as possible".[112] Assuming that Zionism will succeed "in what way will the existence of a small Jewish state in Palestine change anything in the situation of the Polish or German Jews", he asked.[113] Those who believe this to be true are "stricken with an incurable juridical cretinism".[114]
- The impact of Leon's writings on later Left ideologists can be seen from the works of authors like Nathan Weinstock and Maxime Rodinson. Weinstock opposes those reactionaries who "want to preserve artificially the specific Jewish identity".[115] His study is an elaboration of many rehashed arguments like for instance, Zionists' reliance on Antisemitism and its alliance with imperialism. Rodinson's most famous essay, *Israel, Fait Colonial?*

---

110 Walter Laqueur, *A History of Zionism*, New York, 1972, p.433.
111 Abraham Leon, *The Jewish Question. A Marxist Interpretation*, New York, 1970, p. 244.
112 Ibid., p.245.
113 Ibid., p.253.
114 Ibid.
115 Nathan Weinstock, *Zionism: False Messiah*, London, 1979, p.25.

is held by many Antizionists to be one of the best exposition of the thesis on the colonial nature of Zionism.[116]

- Another Trotskysts, Lenni Brenner, bases his attacks on Zionism and the State of Israel on what he calls the "Zionist collusion with Fascists and the Nazis", during the Second World War, which he claims to be substantiating in his book.[117]
- The prominent British Labour Party member Ken Livingstone has said, relying on Brenner's work that "When Hitler won his election in 1932 his policy then was that Jews should be moved to Israel. He was supporting Zionism before he went mad and ended up killing six million Jews".[118]

---

116 Maxime Rodinson, *Israel, Fait Colonial?*, *Les Temps Modernes,* Dossier Le Conflit Israelo-Arabe, no. 253bis, 1967, pp. 17-88.
117 Lenni Brenner, *Zionism in the Age of the Dictators,* London, 1983, p.269.
118 Ken Livingstone, Interview on BBC radio, transcripts in full, The Independent, 28 April, 2016. For a deeper analysis of the British Labour Party's position on Zionism and Israel, see Dave Rich, *The Left's Jewish Problem: Jeremy Corbyn, Israel and Anti-Semitism,* London, 2016. David Hirsh, *Contemporary Left Antisemitism,* London, 2018. Ken Livingstone subsequently resigned from the Labour Party.

Conspiracy Antizionism

- One of the sources of Right-wing attack of Israel and Zionism is the so-called Antisemitic conspiracy theory, the origin of which lies in the *Protocols of the Elders of Zion,* a forged document circulated in Europe at the turn of the century. It consisted of the minutes of the so-called secret deliberations of the leaders of world Jewry plotting to control the destiny of the world. The first Zionist congress in Basle in 1897 was considered the framework for these demonic consultations.[119]
- Conspiracy Antizionism is examined in four groups: Christians, Nazis, Neo-Nazis and Holocaust Deniers.

---

119 Norman Cohn, *Warrant for Genocide, The Myth of the Jewish World Conspiracy and the Protocols of Zion,* London, 1967.

13.

Christian Conspiracy Antizionism

- According to a Christian propagator of the conspiracy theory within the framework of Antizionism, the Jesuit journal *Civilta Cattolica*,

    "The creation of a Jewish state would increase the Jewish menace…[because Jews are] foxy profiteers [who] penetrate into all international organizations… especially into Freemasonry and into the League of Nations".[120]

- According to another source, Gerald Smith, a self-appointed Christian crusader in the United States, "Jew-Zionism is the spearhead of the anti-Christ on this earth, dedicated to the evaporation of the Christian religion, the Christian population and the governmental authority of nations that are predominantly Christian. The enemies of Christ are determined to capture through the United Nations, not through what people call a World Government, but through the manipulating political, financial and military power of World Zionism".

    "I weep and I groan and I pray when I realise how ignorant the American people are concerning what is really going on and how close we are to annihilation, destruction and revolutionary upheaval with the Jew-Zionist machine of the world hovering over us, determined to drain our blood and our purse in the establishment of their Imperial Empire in the counterfeit State of Israel".[121]

---

120 *Civilta Cattolica*, 4 June 1936.
121 Gerald Smith, *The Cross and the Flag*, respectively on 20 March 1973, 19 April 1973 and 7 May 1973, in Arnold Forster and Benjamin R. Epstein,

- Kamal Nasser, is an Anglican, spokesman of the United Command of the Palestinian Revolution, who was killed by Israeli commandos during a raid on Beirut in April 1973.[122] In one sweep, he is able to amalgamate conspiratorial views and his Christian theology with the extraneous ideologies of Marxism in order to attack Zionism:

> "Zionism [is] on a par with imperialism…In the eyes of… those whose faith is linked to the liberation of man from exploitation and slavery [the influence of Zionism is seen as bad] …in relation to the Zionist world domination we are convinced that Zionism has not only be able to infiltrate in the different communities of Western Societies but that it has also been able to penetrate the Christian Church and to submit it in many cases to its desires and cupidity".[123]

The New Anti-Semitism, New York, 1974, p.297.
122 His religious affiliation and tragic death are mentioned by Tony Crow, *The Churches and the Middle East, Christian Action Journal*, special issue on *The Middle East Conflict*, Autumn 1977, p.19. col.1.
123 *Discours pronounce par M. Kamal Nasser, Porte-Parole du Commandement Unifie et de la Revolution Palestinienne, Pour La Palestine, Actes de la Premiere Conference Mondiale des Chretiens pour la Palestine, Beyrouth – Mai 1970*, Paris, 1972, pp. 85-6.

14.

Nazi Conspiracy Antizionism

- The idea of Jewish lust for power has been adopted by Nazi ideology and is basic in its attack on Zionism. The latter is considered as a product and a means of the conspiracy and therefore as wicked.

   "While the Zionists try to make the rest of the world believe that the national consciousness of the Jew finds its satisfaction in the creation of a Palestinian state, the Jews again slyly dupe the dumb Goyim [Gentiles]. It doesn't even enter their heads to build up a Jewish state in Palestine for the purpose of living there; all they want is a central organisation for their international world swindle",

   wrote Hitler in *Mein Kampf*.[124]

- Once the Jewish state is established, the Jews will have a perfectly legal façade behind which they will be able to mask their activities, said the Nazis.

   "The formation of a Jewish State…is not in Germany's interest, since a Palestinian state would not absorb world Jewry but would create an additional position of power under international law for international Jewry, somewhat like the Vatican State for political Catholicism or Moscow for the Comintern",

   wrote von Neurath, German Minister of Foreign Affairs.[125]

---

124 Adolf Hitler, *Mein Kampf*, London 1977, p.294.
125 C. von Neurath, telegram of 1 June 1937 to German representatives in

- Zionists have made agreements with the Antizionist Jews; they cooperate in the development of Palestine. The opposition of religious Jews and Assimilationists to Zionism is a camouflage, wrote Alfred Rosenberg.[126] Zionists and Antizionists are one, wrote Heinz Riecke.[127]
- The Machiavellian aims of the Jewish state are rational, consistent, wrote Heinrich Hest. They are not something new. During the time of King Solomon, the Jews had already succeeded in establishing an empire. The content of the Talmud also reveals these plans. This enterprise is doomed to failure. First because the Jews are not capable of creating a successful state of their own. Secondly, because the Nazis have become aware of their goals and will stop them. It is also not true that Palestine is their homeland, their origins are unknown.[128]
- In short, to sum up, the Nazis considered Zionism as *World Danger*. This was the subtitle to Heinz Riecke's book on Zionism. They, the Nazis, have been able to identify it. What they did to the Jews was seen by them as their contribution to the suppression of Zionism.

Great Britain, Jerusalem and Iraq, *Documents on German Foreign policy 1918-1945,* London, 1953, series D, vol.5, p.746.
126   Alfred Rosenberg, *Der Staatsfeindliche Zionismus,* Munchen, 1938, p.80.
127   Heinz Riecke, *Der Zionismus,* Berlin, 1939, p.61.
128   Heinrich Hest, *Palestina: Judenstaat?,* Berlin, 1939, p.23.

15.

Neo-Nazi Conspiracy Antizionism

- The exposure of the evil of Nazism has not prevented their ideas from being advocated after the Second World War right until today. The British National Front, created in the late sixties, offers a good example of neo-Nazism. It is inspired by mentors such as A.K. Chesterton who offers the following medical analogy:

> "The Arab world has been producing anti-bodies wherewith to resist the implementation in its midst of the Zionist toxin...How far the medical analogy can be taken I do not know...To tell the Arabs...that they must find a modus vivendi with Israel (and here I intend no offense to the Jews) is like telling an organism that it must find a modus vivendi with cancer".[129]

- John Tyndall, a leader of the National Front, in a subtle approach, writes on the subject of the Protocols, that it may be a forgery, but, if so, it is a fiction based on reality, with its popularity as proof of authenticity.[130]
- Martin Webster, another leader of the National Front, writes that the Zionist objective is

> "[t]o keep ordinary Jewish folk in a constant state of hysteria and stampede, so that they could be more ruthlessly squeezed for the continual flood of huge financial dona-

---

129 A.K. Chesterton is quoted by Rosine de Bouneviaille, *Mysterious Mid-East, Candour,* vol.24, no 538-9, October-November 1973, pp. 105-6 and dated as 1967.
130 John Tyndall, *The Jewish Question: Out in the open or under the carpet, Spearhead,* no.89, Mach 1976, p.6.

tions which the Zionist movement needs to keep Israel afloat".[131]

- The National Front has gone so far – perhaps the ultimate in Antizionism - as to claim that Zionists, in order to reach their aim, have staged attacks on their own fellow Jews. For example, it claims that the bomb explosion placed outside a Paris synagogue was timed to go off when all the Jews were inside the building and when only passers-by would be endangered.[132]
- In the wake of the 2014 crisis in Ukraine, the British National Party stated that

  "naive Ukranian nationalists blame Russia for the murder of millions during the 1930s, the Bolsheviks were overwhelmingly not Russian… the radical Jewish racism and supremacism and anti-Christian hatred that in the 1930s produced the Bolshevik terror, now largely find their outlet in the extreme Zionism, anti-white fanaticism and globalism of the neo-cons".[133]

---

[131] Martin Webster, *Media Zionists show their hand, Spearhead*, no.91, May 1976, p.5.

[132] *'Nazi' Terror Scare A Zionist Hoax, National Front News,* no.28, November-December 1980, p.1. See also the editorial in *New Nation*, no.2, Autumn 1980, p.1 and John Tyndall, *Behind the bombings and the wailings, Spearhead,* no.145, November 1980, p.6.

[133] https://www.bnp.org.uk/news/national/ukraine-official-statement, checked on 31 October 2016.

16.

Holocaust Deniers

- Holocaust deniers are unhappy about what they see as the immunity given to Zionism and/or Israel for it deeds, thanks to the Holocaust. To overcome this, they now examine critically the origin of this so-called immunity, the Holocaust, with a view to proving that much of it is not what has really happened, that in fact Zionism/Israel has rewritten the fact in order to get support and immunity for their deeds.
- Paul Rassinier, a French Holocaust survivor, writes about ventures of fabrication and of falsification of historical documents, "one under the social cloak of a Committee for the research into war crimes and war criminals whose head office is in Warsaw, the other under the cloak of the World centre of contemporary Jewish documentation whose two most important branches are in Tel Aviv and in Paris".[134]
- Robert Faurisson, a French university professor, claims that

    > "the so-called 'gas-chambers' and the so-called 'genocide' are one and the same lie...This lie, the origin of which is essentially Zionist, made the gigantic political-financial swindle of which the State of Israel is the chief beneficiary, possible...The chief victims of this lie and swindle are the German people and the Palestinian people".[135]

- Arthur R. Butz, an American, writes that the proof that the genocide is an invention of allied propaganda, especially Jewish and more specifically Zionist propaganda, is that the Jews have

---

134 Paul Rassinier, *Le Drame des Juifs Europeens,* Paris, 1964. p.8.
135 Robert Faurisson, text sent to a number of personalities in Serge Thion, *Verite Historique ou Verite Politique?*, Paris, 1980,.p.93.

a propensity, under the influence of the Talmud, to give imaginary figures.[136]

- Ditlieb Felderer, a Swedish writer, claims that Anne Frank's diary is a "fake used in foisting support for the Zionist gangsterism and to peddle the now so odious Zion-Racism".[137] Adding an element of sexual depravity to the catalogue of Antizionist accusations, Felderer writes that he sees proof of the forgery in that Anne Frank appears to him sexually perverted – seeing in her, features of incipient lesbianism – which he claims, is not the work of Anne Frank but, of someone trying to increase the popularity of the book.[138] It is the "first pornographic work to come out after World War II … the description by a teenage girl over [sic] her sex affairs may likely be the first child porno ever to come out".[139]

---

136 Arthur R. Butz, *The Hoax of the Twentieth Century*, Torrance, 1979, pp. 245-8.
137 *Bible Researcher*, no.160., 1979, p.7, in Ian R. Barnes and Vivienne R.P. Barnes, *A 'Revisionist Historian' Manipulates Anne Frank's Diary, Patterns of Prejudice*, vol.15, no.1, January 1981, p.27.
138 Ditlieb Felderer, Anne Frank's Diary. A Hoax, 1979, pp.10-1, in Barnes, op.cit., p.31.
139 Felderer, ibid., p.64, in ibid.

Christian Antizionism

- Christian Antizionist ideology is the explanation and justification for this type of Antizionism.
- Christianity is complex, fractionalised into different churches with some of them espousing an Antizionist view. The opposition to Zionism and the State of Israel is based on various Christian theological considerations.

17.

"Deicide"

- Above anything else, Jews are blamed for the crime of deicide. Christians consider that it was the Jews who were responsible for the death of Jesus Christ. It is mainly on this basis that the Church has persecuted the Jews. This has been the most powerful and widespread agent in the history of Antisemitism.[140] Zionism being the product of Jews, it is opposed by Christians, just like Judaism, also for deicidal reasons.
- An example of Catholic Antizionism motivated by the argument of deicide can be found in a memorandum forwarded in 1924 by the Italian Christian Association for the Defence of the Holy Places to the Italian government and the League of Nations. The document started with the reference to the *"filthy Jewish rabble; the race of murderers of the Lord"* who have begun to invade the Holy land and went on to argue that Zionism should be stopped.[141]
- *Christian Century,* an American Protestant weekly, wrote in its editorial that Jesus

> "had a programme for Israel which ran counter to the cherished nationalism of Israel's leaders – political and priestly. He opposed their nationalism with the universalism of God's love and God's kingdom".

Jew's ambition was to make Israel and Israel's God the dominant power of the world, but Jesus, by his teaching, threatened this ambition and

---
140   Leon Ploliakov, *Histoire de l'antisemitisme,* Paris, 1955, 1961, 1968, 1977.
141   Pinhas Lapide, *Three Popes and the Jews,* New York, 1967, p.91.

> "[c]ame into collision with Israel's rulers [who considered him as [a] seditious person, a menace to their fantastic nationalism, and to their vested rights and prestige".[142]

- Antizionist Christians have accused the Zionists of actually having crucified the Palestinians. Here their opposition to a Jewish state does not rise out of the far distant past, it derives from the contemporary Arab-Israeli conflict. According to Maximos V Hakim, the Patriach of Antioch and all the Orient, of Alexandria and of Jerusalem, the holder of the highest position in the Greek-Catholic hierarchy in the region

  > "[t]he Arab people of Palestine…[has] become, since more than 50 years, the new lamb of God, flouted and crucified".[143]

---

142 *Christian Century,* 3 May 1933.
143 *Message de Sa Beatitude Maximos V Hakim, Conference Mondiale des Chretiens pour la Palestine, Cahier du Temoignage Chretien,* no.52, Paris, p.22.

18.

"Non-belief"

- Zionism is also opposed on the basis of the non-belief of Jews in the Christian religion. A significant foundation of Christian theology is the idea of spreading itself as much as possible in the world by Christianizing mankind. The liberation of man or woman is only considered as possible in a world where all men and woman have chosen to follow Christ. This belief has been used in the framework of Antizionism. The state of Israel, when established, would represent an achievement and symbol of the Jewish unbelievers, an anti-thesis, an obstacle to the universal mission of the Church and is therefore opposed.
- In January 23 1904, Theodor Herzl, the founder of modern Zionism, was granted an audience with the Vatican's Secretary of State, Cardinal Merry del Val. His position was as follows:

  > "As long as the Jews deny the divinity of Christ, we certainly cannot make a declaration in their favour… they deny the divine nature of Christ. How then can we, without abandoning our highest principles, agree to their being given possession of the Holy Land again…in order for us to come out for the Jewish people in the way they desire, they would first have to be converted".[144]

- Three days later, Herzl had an audience with Pope Pius X who merely reiterated the same argument:

  > "We cannot give approval to this movement. We cannot prevent the Jews from going to Jerusalem – but we could never

---

144 *The Complete Diaries of Theodor Herzl*, R. Patai ed., London, 1960, vol.4, pp. 1593-4.

sanction it. The soil of Jerusalem, if not always sacred, has been sanctified by the life of Jesus Christ. As the head of the Church I cannot tell anything different. The Jews have not recognized our Lord, therefore we cannot recognize the Jewish people [and its aspiration to a national existence]".[145]

- Christianity, it is claimed, is superior over other religions. "The Jewish religion, like any other religion, is an alien element", according to *Christian Century*.[146] The Jews should abandon any distinctiveness as Jews and in the framework of a separate national existence. "A simple gesture of recognition would be the unconstrained observance of Jesus' birthday".[147] Should this not happen, a threat is levelled: "the spirit of tolerance would shrivel up"[148], "the prejudice and anger…will flame up to their great hurt".[149]

---

145 Ibid., pp. 1602-3.
146 *Christian Century,* 7 July 1937.
147 Ibid., 20 December 1939.
148 Ibid., 29 April 1936.
149 Ibid., 9 June 1937.

19.

Other Christian Arguments

- **Temporariness** The existence of the Jews is seen as temporary. It is claimed that the reading of the Holy Books makes it appear that there is a constant renewal, that there can be no permanent achievement. The state of Israel is then opposed because of the claim that Israel is an everlasting phenomenon and this is considered as contrary to the temporary values which Christian theology affirms. The essence of Jesus message

    > "[s]hows that there is always a new future possibility for man. Nothing can be settled, fixed…There is no Holy Land. There can be no Zionism based on the Bible if the Gospel really is the book that calls to a constant renewal".[150]

- **Replacement** Another argument is that the promise made in the Old Testament to the Jewish People has been transformed by the New Testament so that the promise of the land is repaced by Jesus' personification of the land. In *Pour La Palestine*, Georges Khodre, writes that

    > "Jesus announces the Kingdom of God…The word earth disappears, that of heirs subsists. The promise is fulfilled in the Christ. He personally represents the heritage".[151]

---

150 Philippe Marty, *La Bible, un Livre Seculier, Pour la Palestine, Actes de la Premiere Conference Mondiale des Chretiens pour la Palestine, Beyrouth – Mai 1970,* Paris, 1972, pp.76-7.

151 Georges Khodre, *Le Sens de la Promesse de la Terre selon la Foi Chretienne, Pour La Palestine,* ibid., p.48.

- **Divine act** The re-establishment of the State of Israel, runs another argument, can only be brought about through a divine act. The secretary of the World Conference of Christians for Palestine complains about the Jews "who want to put an end to the exile by the help of human means".[152] For him, Zionism is thus an act of defiance of God's will and cannot therefore be supported.
- **New Testament quotes** Several arguments are substantiated with quotations from the New Testament. In a memorandum, a group of Middle east Christian theologians of various denominations wrote:

   "As for the land, this is a kingdom of Heaven and it will be inherited through the Holy Spirit. (Beatitudes, Matthew 5). To understand the promise made to Abraham in the material sense is to pervert God's plan. It is only in the spiritual sense that this promise can be fulfilled, by Christ arisen (Acts.13.32)".[153]

- **Election** According to another argument, Jews have been chosen by God to serve as an example of heavenly destiny, to reveal to all the world God's presence and plans. If Jews are to serve all of humanity for such purpose, then their presence cannot be restricted to a region and in such a particular form of society as the state. Jews are a people chosen by God

   "in order to reveal his plan for the salvation of humanity in Christ… The Jewish people have been called to live out in their own history, the history of the whole of humanity. A history in which God saves man. It is because of this that they are not people with any temporal or political destiny but exist as an example to all of their heavenly destiny".[154]

---

152 Georges Montaron, *Discours d'Ouverture, Pour la Palestine,* ibid., p.23.
153 Jean Corbon, Georges Khodr, Samir Kafeety and Albert Laham, *What is Required of the Christian Faith Concerning the Palestine Problem, Christians, Zionism and Palestine,* Anthology Series no.4, The Institute of Palestine Studies, Beirut, 1970, p.73.
154 Ibid., p.72.

- **Millenarians** Millenarian Christians have held the belief that a return of the Jewish People to their homeland and the restoration of their rule, would be the precondition for the return of Jesus and the establishment of the world rule of Christianity. Needless to say, Judaism and the Jewish state would have to disappear, according to this vision. It is an attitude which in essence is Antizionist but in the short term and as a means to the final goal is pro-Zionist. It can be found for example, amongst Russian Orthodox Christians who viewed Zionism positively.[155]
- **Violence** Some Christian Antizionists justify the use of violence in order to reach their aims. Witness the following conclusions adopted by the Theological Commission of the Beirut 1970 World Conference of Christians for Palestine:

    "We have...been brought to recognize the fact of a 'liberating' violence that challenges Christian consciousness, as a reply to original violence established by the will of power, vain gloriousness and material superiority".[156]

- **Holocaust Denial and Conspiracy Theories** The Reverend Sizer, a British Church of England Vicar, has used his website to link to Antisemitic material from other websites. In 2014 Sizer participated as a panellist at an Antisemitic conference in Iran which included Holocaust Deniers and conspiracy theorists and whose declared aim was to "unveil the secrets behind the dominance of the Zionist Lobby over US and EU Politics".[157]
- **Ideology of the Left** Christian Antizionists also rely on the ideology of the left[158] which is foreign to Christian teaching, in their opposition to Zionism. The reliance by Christians is

---

155 *Church Herald*, 1902, in Mikhail Agursky, *Some Russian Orthodox Reaction to Early Zionism: 1900-1914, Christian Jewish Relations*, no.73, December 1980, pp. 54-5.
156 *Rapport de la Commission Theologique, Pour la Palestine*, op.cit. p.362.
157 https://cst.org.uk/news/blog/2014/10/02/rev-stephen-sizer-speaking-at-antisemitic-conference-in-iran, checked on 1 November, 2016.
158 See for example the statement of the Greek-Catholic Bishop of Aleppo, his Lordship Edelby, *Temoignage Chretien*, 26 April 1973.

paradoxical having in mind the traditional opposition of Christianity to this ideology and the specific complaint directed at Zionism and Israel leaders by Christians that it was under the influence of Communism.[159]

---

159 *La Croix*, 20 November 1948.

Jewish Antizionism

- Jewish Antizionist ideology is the explanation and justification for this type of Antizionism.
- Jewish Antizionists are not a homogeneous group. There were three main different ideological attitudes. Emancipationist, Orthodox and Left Antizionism. The first two will be examined here. Left Antizionism has been examined above.[160]

---

160   See pp. 27-50.

20.

Emancipationism[161]

- Emancipationist Antizionism was a consequence of the era of Enlightenment in the 17th and 18th centuries in the West, when a new political and social order emerged, influenced by ideals of freedom and equality for all. Jews benefitted from this movement in varying degrees.
- Antizionism was advocated by Jews who sought to assimilate into gentile society, a feature called "self-hatred". Those Jews had great hopes in the new world that was opening its gates to them thanks to the Enlightenment, and every impediment to the assimilation of Jews – including Zionism – was considered by them anathema.
- A similar Antizionism was also advocated by those Jews who wanted to integrate in Gentile society, while maintaining completely or with some reform their Jewish identity.
- The Emancipationists did not accept the Zionist view that a nation where Jews would live out their own destiny without Gentile interference was the best antidote to persecution. They were absolutely convinced that Antisemitism was on the way to being eliminated from the world, that the forces of Enlightenment were much stronger than those of Antisemitism and would overcome it.
- Emancipationists believed that hatred was motivated by the specificity which Jews stubbornly had maintained over the years and that once the Jews would be emancipated, the phenomenon of Antisemitism would disappear. Zionism, they thought, also represented a defeatist approach because instead of fighting against evil, it proposed to abandon the battleground to the enemy and to escape to Palestine. This is in fact a form of fatalism,

---

161 This section is based on Walter Laqueur, op.cit., p. 385-407.

an acknowledgement of failure and would merely encourage Jew-haters in their endeavour.
- The accusation of dual loyalty was also levelled. In a letter to *The Times*, David Alexander and Claude Montefiore, respectively Presidents of the Board of Deputies of British Jews (the national representative body of the UK Jewish community) and the Anglo-Jewish Association, expressed the view that the Emancipationists fully identified with the country of which they were citizens, they were good patriots sharing the national consciousness of their homeland. The assumption that the Jews are "incapable of complete social and political identification with the nations among which they dwell" was everything but right.[162]
- Pursuing this matter even further, Emancipationists said they felt a genuine admiration for the culture of their respective countries. "I do not read Faust as a beautiful poem", wrote the German philosopher Hermann Cohen, "I love it as a revelation of the German spirit. I feel in a similar way even about Luther, about Mozart and Beethoven, Stein and Bismark".[163] Zionism, it was held, on the other hand, had no culture.
- The assertion that the Jews did not form a nation was also often advanced as an argument, because according to that view, only a nation was entitled to a state of its own.
- Zionism as a form of nationalism was very much criticised as it was considered that nationalism had done more harm than good.
- Several Emancipationists who had succeeded in obtaining very satisfactory political or social positions in Gentile society, saw in Zionism a threat to their position or would-be position. Moreover, "how could the European countries which the Jews proposed to 'abandon' justify their retention of the Jews? Why should civil equality have been won by the strenuous exertions of the Jews if the Jews themselves were to be the first to offer to 'evacuate' their position and to claim bare courtesy of 'foreign

---

162 *The Times*, 24 May 1927.
163 Hermann Cohen, *Antwort auf das Offene Schreiben des Herrn Dr Martin Buber an Hermann Cohen, K.C. – Blatter*, no.12, July – August 1916, p.13.

visitors'?" [164] Ludwig Geiger, in Germany, appealed to concrete measures: Zionist should be deprived of their civic rights.[165]

- Other arguments were that Zionism was racist, based on the idea of the specificity of Jews, which in turn was based on consanguinity, that it could be compared in its evil to Nihilism, Communism and the right, that the fate of the Jewish people was to live in exile, dispersion and persecution, that Zionism was a political phenomenon and therefore opposed to the spiritual character of Judaism, and that Herzl was a false prophet like Shabtai Zvi.

---

164 Laurie Magnus, *Zionism and the Neo-Zionists,* London, 1917, p.6.
165 Ludwig Geiger, *Zionismus und Deutschtun, Die Stimme Der Wahrheit,* L. Schon and N. Philippi eds., Wurzburg, 1905, p.168.

21.

Protest Rabbis

- The Zionist idea for very religious Jews was in contradiction with Judaism as it represented a disbelief in the existence of God and was in contradiction to the Jewish religious laws.
- A number of Antizionist Rabbis energetically engaged in a forceful campaign to prove their point. They were called the Protest Rabbis, a label coined by Theodor Herzl, the founder of modern Zionism, in relation to the signatories of a press release by five German Rabbis. When the first Zionist Congress was planned to be held in 1897, German Rabbis, in the name of the Association of Rabbis in Germany, an Antizionist organisation including representatives of different wings of Judaism, published a fierce attack on Zionism from a religious point of view.
- In their statement, the Rabbis argued that the efforts to found a national state in Palestine contradicted the messianic promises of Judaism as contained in the Holy Writ and in later religious sources. Furthermore, it was claimed that Judaism obligates its adherents to serve "with all devotion the Fatherland to which they belong, and to further its national interests with all their heart and with all their strength". The statement added that there was no objection to the colonization of Palestine by Jewish peasants and farmers so long as they have no relation to the founding of a national state.[166]
- The press release elicited various reactions. Herzl wrote an article in *Die Welt* on July 16, 1897, where he called these Antizionist Rabbis "Protestrabbiner" and the Zionist Congress, originally planned for Munich, was moved to Basel.[167]

---

166   Press release by the 'Protest Rabbis', in Theodor Herzl, *A Portrait for this Age*, L. Lewisohn ed., New York, 1955, pp.304-5.
167   Tamara Zieve, *This Week in History: Herzl, Rabbis Clash on Zionism*, The

22.

Protest Rabbis Followers

- The five Antizionist German Rabbis were to be followed by numerous other Rabbis. In 1902, a collection of letters of more than 50 Rabbis was published in Warsaw in Hebrew by Rabbi Abraham Baruch Steinberg and this represents probably the most important single source for the study of the Protest Rabbis movement.
- The fundamental assertion about Zionism was that it represented a denial of God and a violation of the Jewish religious laws. The latter being the product of God, the non-respect of the law was also perceived as a denial of God. Zionists "withdraw their belief in the Lord", wrote Rabbi Steinberg in his introduction.[168]
- The Rabbis argued that the Bible did call to every believer to settle in the Holy land, the "Mitzvath Yishuv Eretz Israel", but this return was to be made on the Day of Redemption, when the Messiah would come.[169] In other words, the return would have to be a divine act and it could therefore not be the product of man's hand. This made it appear that there was a consensus between the Zionists and those Rabbis; their ultimate aim was the same, Jews could return to Zion and the House of Israel would be re-established. It was in relation to the means that their view differed. Whereas for the Zionists this could be done by themselves, for those Rabbis, this was sacrilege, a profanation of the Lord's will and the Holy books.

Jerusalem Post, 15 July 2012.
168 *Sefer Daath Harabanim,* A.B. Steinberg ed., Warsaw, 1902. The book is divided in two part with the second part starting with a new pagination; the first part will be referred to as A and the second part as B.
169 Ibid, B, p.37.

- The Antizionist Rabbis also claimed that the Zionists were in fact "Nevieh Sheker" i.e. false prophets who like their predecessors were exploiting the gullibility of the masses by their deceit.

  > "All the prophecies predicted by Jeremiah, the prophet, in relation to the people of his generation who were lured and trapped by the false prophets, can be seen now in the last generation by the rise of the Zionist billow"

  wrote Rabbi Steinberg.[170]

- Rabbi Steinberg also asserted that the same fates that occurred in Biblical times to those who did not follow the way shown by God, will happen to the advocates of the Jewish state. He draws the attention to the story of Manasseh, son of Hezekiah, and asserts that his worshipping of idols brought about God's punishment upon him, his descendant and his people.[171]
- These Antizionist Rabbis saw themselves possibly as the saviours of Israel, the men on whom the duty had fallen to bring the sinners on to the right path:

  > "It is a good deed to save these [Zionist] souls…only when they will vanish and end [their enterprises] will happiness sprout, then Israel will be blessed and will multiply as the stars in the sky".[172]

---

170 *Sefer Daath Harabanim,* ibid., A, p.5.
171 Ibid., A, p.30.
172 Rabbi Nata, in *Sefer Daath Harabanim,* op.cit., B, p.51.

23.

Breuer and Agudath Israel

- Agudath Israel was established in 1912, mainly to oppose the Zionists. It has been the leading organisation of Orthodox Antizionists. Isaac Breuer, 1883-1946, was an important figure in Agudath Israel.[173]
- Breuer's main reproach against the Zionists was their secularism. His opposition in 1926 to a plan by the Va'ad Leoumi, the National Council of Palestinian Jewry, laying down the framework of the Jewish Home was that it "ignores God and the Torah [Old Testament]. They are not mentioned at all".[174] There is not "a word, not a sign of the Jewish nation's incomparable originality during four thousand years".[175]
- Referring to the separation of secular from religious matter, Breuer writes that the plan

    "is so radical, a break with the whole of the Jewish past… The Jewish nation will have ceased to be God's nation from the moment it accepts the separation".[176]

The only references to religious practices in the above plan i.e. the provision of slaughterhouses, the actual ritual slaughter and the flat unleavened bread, give the impression that only the latter were God's province, that the main consideration is food

---

173 *Encyclopaedia Judaica,* Jerusalem, 1973, vol.4, pp.1364-5.
174 Isaac Breuer's opposition to the Draft Ordinance of the Va'ad Leoumi, the National Council of Palestinian Jewry can be found in his book, *The Jewish National Home,* Frankfort-On-the-Maine, 1926, p.71.
175 Ibid.
176 Ibid., p.75.

and "that God and the Torah claimed no interest".[177] Zionists are guilty of "malice, unfairness, uncharitableness, intolerance, callousness and abuse of power".[178]

- Over time Agudath Israel has come a long way closer to the Zionist camp. It is a political party whose representatives have been regularly elected to the Israeli Parliament and it has even joined ruling Government coalitions.[179]

---

177 Ibid., p.79.
178 Ibid., p.67.
179 https://www.knesset.gov.il/faction/eng/FactionPage_eng.asp?PG=22, checked on 8 January 2018.

24.

Neturei Karta

- Neturei Karta is a small, ultra-orthodox sect living mainly in Jerusalem - the name of Neturei Karta is Aramaic for "Guardians of the City" – who broke away from Agudath Israel in 1935. It has lived in separation from the rest of Israeli society but has been tolerated as such by the state.[180]
- Its ideology, in addition to the classical religious Antizionist arguments, is most radical. It has asserted that it will never accept the State of Israel, even if Arabs do[181], has expressed willingness to ally itself with the Palestine Liberation Organisation[182] and has even called, in its resistance to state tax collection, for the killing of the tax collectors as it has claimed that this is sanctioned by religious law.[183]
- Its articulate American supporters, based in Brooklyn, have engaged in diverse activities. They have sent letters to the United Nations Secretary-General, stressing Zionist "fraud, deception and usurpation"[184] and published books such as *Min Hameitsar* by Rabbi Michael Dov Weissmandel[185] and *The Holocaust Victims Accuse* by Rabbi Moshe Shonfeld[186] purporting to show that the Zionists have much to be reproached with for the Holocaust of the Second World War.
- Members of London's Stamford Hill branch of the *Neturei Karta* have told an audience that

---

180 *Encyclopaedia Judaica*, op. cit., vol.12, pp. 1002-3
181 *Yediot Aharonot*, 21 February 1975.
182 Ibid.
183 *The Jerusalem Post International Edition*, 2-8 November 1980.
184 *United Nations General Assembly*, 30th Session, 1975, Agenda item 68, A/10341, Annex.
185 Michael Dov Weissmandel, *Min Hameitsar*, Brooklyn, 1960.
186 Reb Moshe Shonfeld, *The Holocaust Victims Accuse*, Brooklyn, 1977.

"The majority of Jews in Europe before the war were religious. The Zionist thought it worthwhile to have the majority of these people murdered in the gas chambers in order to prevent them founding the State of Israel".[187]

---

187 *Jewish Chronicle*, 17 April 1981.

Arab and Muslim Antizionism

- Arab and Muslim Antizionist ideology is the explanation and justification for this type of Antizionism.
- Arab and Muslim Antizionism are not homogeneous. The main driving force of Arab and Muslim Antizionism is based in the Middle East and includes the so-called Rejectionists of any accommodation with Israel. This group includes Iran, the Muslim Brotherhood, Hezbollah, Hamas and the Islamic State (ISIS). However, it is also found amongst non-Rejectionists Arabs and Muslims based in the Middle East. Another driving force consists of Arabs and Muslims based in the West.
- This ideology is very complex and includes an almost infinite number of arguments explaining and justifying the attitude. It is analysed in the following sections: Aims, Libels, Islam, "Imperialism/Colonialism", "Apartheid" and Boycott, Divestment, Sanctions (BDS).
- Considerable research has been undertaken in the Palestinian and Arab ideology in the Conflict. Those interested will find the most thorough information and analysis - over and above the small representative selection given in this handbook - in *Palestine Media Watch* and *Middle East Media Research Institute*.[188]

---

188 https://www.palwatch.org/; https://www.memri.org/

25.

Aims

- Arab and Muslim Antizionism is an ideology that opposes Zionism and the State of Israel. Politicidal Antizionism aims to bring an end to the existence of the State of Israel. Anti-Israel Antizionism aims at delegitimizing, dehumanizing and demonizing Israel.
- Statements of the Politicidal Antizionism and its Anti-Israel Antizionism corollary is a permanent and widespread feature of Palestinian and wider Arab and Muslim societies as expressed through official spokesmen, the media, culture, the education curriculum and various civil organisations.
- Sometimes the goal is expressed in explicit language but often the objective is presented in a more indirect, ambiguous way as a camouflage because it arouses some discomfort to the intended audiences. Below a representative sample of explicit statements.

> "Arab unity means the liquidation of Israel and the expansionist dreams of Zionism".[189]

> "Interviewer: How do you read the future of the peace process? Al-Hourani: Whether they (the Israelis) return to negotiations or not, and whether they fulfil the agreements or not - the political plan is a temporary agreement, and the conflict remains eternal, will not come to an end and the agreements being talked about are in the context of the current balance of power. As to the struggle, it will continue. It may pause at times, but in the final analysis, Palestine is ours from the [Mediterranean] Sea to the [Jordan] River".[190]

---

189 Gamal Abdel Nasser Hussein, President of Egypt, at the Festival of Unity, 22 February 1965, in Y. Harkabi, op. cit., p.2.
190 Al-Hourani, Head of Political Committee of the Palestinian National

"The revolution is still continuing until this day, and that is what members of the Palestinian people are translating [into action] by their resistance to the Zionist enemy with knives. We will pursue you [Zionists] with car rammings and kill you with rocks, Allah willing, and we will defeat you, and through intelligence, culture, and art, we will hold you accountable. We are a people that is worthy of living and you are a people whose fate is to disappear".[191]

"Imam Khomeini continued to warn against the Zionist regime and its supporters to his very last day, and later, the most senior echelon in the Islamic Republic continued with these warnings and with the policy of fighting the danger posed by Israel and its supporters… It is, therefore, necessary to continue the policy of struggle until Israel is eradicated from the region. When Imam Khomeini firmly declared that Israel must be wiped off the world's map, some may have had difficulty accepting this policy. Today, however, everyone understands that there is no alternative for this occupying regime other than this fate".[192]

Council, Official PA daily, Al-Hayat Al-Jadida, Apr. 14, 2001, http://www.palwatch.org/main.aspx?fi=449&all=1, checked on 12 May 2017.

191 Tawfiq Abdallah, Fatah Head of Information in Tyre, Lebanon, 15 January 2017, Falestinona, website of Fatah's Information and Culture Commission in Lebanon, 2 March 2017, http://www.palwatch.org/main.aspx?fi=449, checked on 12 May 2017.

192 *Jomhouri-ye Eslami*, affiliated with Ali Akbar Hashemi Rafsanjani, the chairman of the Expediency Council and the patron of President Hassan Rohani, 20 July 2014, https://www.memri.org/reports/iranian-reactions-war-gaza-israels-destruction-imminent-israel-attacks-due-arab-worlds#_edn3, checked on 12 May 2017.

26.

Libels

- There is a rich catalogue of scurrilous libels brought by Arabs/Muslims against Zionism and the State of Israel. Amongst them are the depiction of Israel as a cancer, a disease spreading Aids, the accusation that Israelis are stealing organs from Palestinians, the blood libel i.e. the accusation that Israel is using blood from non-Jews for ritual purposes, the use of the conspiracy theme of the *Protocols of the Elders of Zion*, the equation with Nazi crimes and Holocaust denial.

    "The only way to save the region is to remove from the body this cancer that is Israel, which is the reason for all the types of backwardness and destruction".[193]

    "Egypt is always flooded with Israeli food products and fruits, 60-70% of which are drowning in chemicals. This is very clear. There are 200,000 cases of kidney failure in Upper Egypt. 200,000 people receive dialysis treatment. This is because of the Israeli agricultural carcinogenic medicine, which has been imported for the past 7-8 years by the greedy 'Knights of Normalization,' whose only allegiance is to their pockets. This caused 200,000 cases [of kidney failure], and they are the statistics of last year. This year, the number is definitely higher. Let's not even mention the AIDS girls that they are sending there, or the [EgyptAir] plane coming from the U.S., which they downed, sending 90 Egyptian generals to the sharks. This Israel, this Zionism, kills more in times of peace than in wartime".[194]

---

193 Abbas Zaki, Fatah Central Committee Member, *Al-Mayadeen* TV program, 22 November 2015, http://palwatch.org/main.aspx?fi=760, checked on 14 April 2017.

194 Ismail Sukariyya, Hizbullah MP on Syrian TV, 19 December 2010, https://

"The rabbis in Israel forbid the Jews in Israel and in the world to give up their organs when they die, and based on the tenets of their faith, [which appear] in the Talmud, they believe that removing organs from the bodies of Jews is a violation of the religious laws. That is why the [Israeli] hospitals, and especially the commanders of the Israeli army, call to obtain organs in another way, not from Jews... Some rabbis who are considered relatively moderate have permitted to transplant organs taken from a non-Jew in the body of a Jew...With the advent of advanced medical machinery, surgery [procedures] and medications, organ trafficking has become a prevalent [phenomenon] in the world, and that is why Israel can traffic in organs at the Palestinians' expense, and thanks to the presence of the occupation army among [the Palestinians]".[195]

"During the 1830s... Damascus was shocked by a terrible crime - the priest Tomas Al-Kaboushi fell victim to a group of Jews who sought to drain his blood to prepare baked goods for their Yom Kippur holiday [sic]... The 1840 incident recurred several times in the 20th century when the Zionists carried out the mass crimes in Palestine and Lebanon – acts that shocked the conscience of good people all over the world and were condemned by world public opinion. But each time, the Zionist financial, media, and political influence managed to pacify the anger and distract the people from these crimes. Instead of being punished, the Zionists received a reward...: great financial aid and horrifying stockpiles of advanced weaponry".[196]

---

www.memri.org/reports/hizbullah-mp-ismail-sukariyya-syrian-tv-accuses-israel-sending-egypt-agricultural, checked on 14 April 1917.

195 Tahsin Al-Halabi, *Al-Watan* (Syria), 25 August 2009, https://www.memri.org/reports/arab-reactions-aftonbladet-report-accusing-israel-trafficking-palestinians-organs, checked on 14 April 2017.

196 Field Marshal Mustafa Tlass, previous Syrian Defence Minister, https://www.memri.org/reports/damascus-blood-libel-1840-told-syrian-defense-minister-mustafa-tlass, checked on 14 April 2017.

"Hamas is calling upon the Arab and Islamic peoples to act seriously and tirelessly in order to frustrate that dreadful scheme ... Today it is Palestine and tomorrow it may be another country or other countries. For Zionist scheming has no end, and after Palestine they will covet expansion from the Nile to the Euphrates... Their scheme has been laid out in The Protocols of the Elders of Zion, and their present [conduct] is the best proof of what is said there".[197]

"Palestinian Liberation Front (i.e., a PLO faction) political bureau member Muhammad Al-Soudi emphasized that the incessant crimes of the occupation necessitate action on the international level in order to put the occupation and its leaders on trial for committing crimes more serious than the crimes of fascism and Nazism".[198]

"It seems that the interest of the Zionist movement, however, is to inflate this figure [six million Jews murdered in the Holocaust] so that their gains will be greater…a partnership was established between Hitler's Nazis and the leadership of the Zionist movement ... [the Zionists gave] permission to every racist in the world, led by Hitler and the Nazis, to treat Jews as they wish, so long as it guarantees immigration to Palestine". The Zionist leaders actually "wanted" Jews to be murdered, because "having more victims meant greater rights and stronger privilege to join the negotiation table for dividing the spoils of war once it was over".[199]

---

197 1988 Hamas Charter, Article 32, http://palwatch.org/main.aspx?fi=783, checked on 14 April 2017

198 Muhammad Al-Soudi, Al-Hayat Al-Jadida, 11 January 2017, http://palwatch.org/main.aspx?fi=808, checked on 14 April 1917.

199 Mahmoud Abbas, the President of the Palestinian Authority, in a book published in Arabic in 1983 and titled *The Other Side: The Secret Relations Between Nazism and the Leadership of the Zionist Movement*, originally his doctoral dissertation, completed at Moscow Oriental College, in the Soviet Union, according to a translation of the text provided by the Simon Wiesenthal Center, in *A Holocaust-Denier as Prime Minister of "Palestine"* by Dr. Rafael Medoff, http://www.wymaninstitute.org/articles/2003-03-denier.php,

- According to the American Reverend Louis Farrakhan, the Nation of Islam leader,

    "we now know that the crime they say is at the root of terrorism was not committed by Arabs or Muslims at all …It is now becoming apparent that there were many Israelis and Zionist Jews in key roles in the 9/11 attacks…We're dealing with thieves and liars and murderers. …We know that many Israelis were arrested immediately after the attacks, but quickly released and sent to Israel…We know that an Israeli film crew dressed as Arabs were filming the Twin Towers before the first plane went in. In other words, these Israelis had full knowledge of the attacks…We know that many Jews received a text message not to come to work on September 11th. Who sent that message that kept them from showing up?... And we know that Benjamin Netanyahu told an audience in Israel, we are benefitting from one thing and that is the attack on the Twin Towers and Pentagon and the American struggle in Iraq. He added that these catastrophes and wars would swing the American public opinion in the favor of Israel".[200]

---

checked on 1 November 2016.
200 *The Reverend Louis Farrakhan, the Nation of Islam leader, Louis Farrakhan: 'Israelis and Zionist Jews' played key roles in 9/11 attacks*, Jessica Chasmar, *The Washington Times*, 5 March 2015, http://www.washingtontimes.com/news/2015/mar/5/louis-farrakhan-israelis-and-zionist-jews-played-k/, checked on 19 December 2016.

27.

Islam

- Islam plays an important role in Arab and Muslim Antizionism. Islam is basically an expansionist religion that divides the world in two: "Dar al-Islam", "The Abode of Islam" and "Dar al-Harb", "The Abode of War". The latter refers to those parts of the world that do not accept the sole authority of Islam and against which Muslims must wage a "Jihad", a "Holy War", a collective duty of Muslim faithful, until the whole world becomes "Dar al-Islam".[201]
- With regards to non-Islamic communities such as the Jews living in Islamic countries, Islam considered those as tolerated on the condition that they submitted to the Islamic authorities.[202] Their status was known as "Dhimmis", so-called protected communities who were allowed to keep their properties and to practice their religion but had to submit to a discriminated status.[203]
- The Quran contains numerous Antisemitic passages and this has had a major influence on the image of the Jews in the eyes of the Muslim/Arab population.[204]
- Arab/Muslim attitudes to Zionism/Israel are laced with Islamic themes that play a role in the articulation, justification and strengthening of that attitude. Amongst some of the main themes are that the Jewish state represents a provocation to the edicts, rule and destiny of Islam, to the Islamic attachment to Palestine and that Antizionism is legitimate given

---

201 Harkabi, op. cit. p.132.
202 Ibid.
203 Efraim Karsh, *Islamic Imperialism, A History*, New Haven, 2006, pp.25-26. See also Bat Ye'or, *The Dhimmi: Jews and Christians under Islam*, Rutherford, 1985.
204 Harkabi, op.cit. pp.220-223. For passages referring to Jews in the Quran, see http://www.jewishvirtuallibrary.org/references-to-jews-in-the-koran, checked on 25 April 2017.

the demonic nature and ambitions of the Jews as depicted by Islam.[205]

"The problem of Palestine is religious and hatred, and any attempts to deal with it which is not based on a religious Jihad is doomed to failure. There is no alternative…The leaders of the secular Arab parties ignore the fact that in all the decisive historic battles of Arabism and Islam…the battle-cry was religious and sacred: Allah Akbar [God is Great]".[206]

"Let me be clear. Jihad is the only way to resolve this issue. With the Jews, one cannot achieve anything by means of peace, or a settlement, or open borders, or diplomatic and commercial ties. They are devils in human form. Many people think that Judaism is a religion, but today's Jews are not really Jews, and have nothing to do with Moses and the Torah. They are a gang of evil thieves who stole this land. By nature, a thief who knows he has no right to the land imposes his presence by means of force, by bloodshed, by excessive massacres, by excessive killings, and by destruction, in order to prove that he has rights in this region".[207]

"O, you who were brought up on spilling blood
O, you who murdered Allah's pious prophets
You have been condemned to humiliation and hardship
O Sons of Zion, O most evil among creations
O barbaric apes, O wretched pigs".[208]

---

205 https://www.palwatch.org/ and https://www.memri.org/
206 Abdallah al-Tall, *The Danger of World Jewry to Islam and Christianity*, Cairo, 1964, pp.8-10, in Harkabi, op.cit., p.136.
207 Egyptian cleric Zaghloul Al-Naggar, Al-Rahma TV, 6 January 2009, https://www.memri.org/reports/egyptian-cleric-zaghloul-al-naggar-arab-world-ruled-scum-earth-and-garbage-all-nations-i-am. See video clip on http://www.memri.org/legacy/clip/2033, checked on 14 April 2017.
208 Official PA TV, 12 September 2014, https://www.palwatch.org/main.aspx?fi=1061&page=6, checked on 25 April 2017. See also video, ibid.

"The Meccan [Quran] chapter entitled 'Jews' or 'Children of Israel' is remarkable... It's about today's Jews, those of our century, and speaks only of extermination and digging graves... This chapter sentences the Jews to extermination before a single Jew existed on earth... Palestine's blessing is linked to destruction of the center of global corruption [Jews of Israel], the snake's head. When the snake's head of [global] corruption is cut off, here in Palestine, and when the octopus' [Jew's] tentacles are cut off around the world, the real blessing will come with the destruction of the Jews, here in Palestine, and it is one of the splendid real blessings in Palestine".[209]

---

[209] Hamas cleric on Al-Aqsa TV (Hamas), 13 July 2008, https://www.palwatch.org/main.aspx?fi=1061&page=11, checked on 25 April 2017. See also video in ibid.

28.

"Colonialism/Imperialism"

- One of the most recurring accusations levelled by Arab and Muslim Antizionist ideology (but also by other Antizionist ideologies) is that Zionism/Israel is a colonialist and imperialist implant.
- Ideologues of the Left have claimed that in order to find markets for their surpluses, capitalist nations established colonies in foreign territories, subordinating their native inhabitants and exploiting their resources. Zionism and Israel are seen as the colonialist implant of the imperialist powers.[210]
- In the Antizionist literature, Israel is described as the advance base for imperialism, the starting point for the conquest of the region. Evidence of this theory can be seen in the 1917 Balfour Declaration by Britain, the British Mandate over Palestine between 1922-1948, the Sinai war of 1956, and the political, military and economic support given to Israel by the USA and other Western nations over the years. Israel's territorial expansion following several wars and the growing settlements in the West Bank of Jordan following the 1967 War, are seen as further proof of its expansionist character and the ambitions of imperialist powers.

> "Even Israel itself was but one of the outcomes of imperialism. If it had not fallen under British mandate, Zionism could not have found a necessary support to realize the idea of a national home in Palestine".[211]

> "The relationship between Israel and the U.S. is like the relationship between the mosquito and the malaria microbe.

---

210 See chapter on Left Antizionism, pp. 27-50.
211 Abdel Gamal Nasser, president of Egypt, *Philosophy of the Revolution,* Cairo, undated, p.69, in Harkabi, op. cit., p. 154.

The mosquito's interest is to suck blood, while the microbe's is to corrupt…The malaria microbe settles in the mosquito's stomach and eventually kills it…The malaria microbe deludes it into thinking that its interest is to invade Sudan and carry out recurring invasions, because this is the age of imperialism…When [next] September the ninth [i.e. 9/11] comes, we will again review the material we handed out about the Jewish thumbprint. Let's say in brief that whether the 9/9 [sic] events and the destruction of the two famous buildings in the U.S. were carried out by Israel's enemies, as the U.S. claims, or by Israeli agents, as we claim, the outcome is the same: the Jews are the cause. These Jews hasten America's death. The U.S. must beware…They must understand this now and dismantle this alliance with the Jews".[212]

"Yesterday, the department of political science at Bir Zeit University…held a symposium… Professor Samih Hamouda, of the political science department at Bir Zeit University, presented an analysis of the research papers written by President Mahmoud Abbas on the subject of Zionist ideology. Prof. Hamouda said that in his writings and research, the President linked Zionism to imperialism by examining the reasons for the growth of Zionism, through scientific analysis of European society and the problem of the Jews in Europe, and linking this with the aspirations of the West in the Arabic East. He added, 'In the President's research, the Zionist movement is not Jewish, nor does it flow from the desires of the Jews themselves. Rather, it is an imperialist colonialist movement which sought to use the Jews and to enlist them to further the western colonialist plans'".[213]

---

212 Sheikh Abd Al-Jalil Al-Khouri, imam of the Shahid Mosque in Khartoum as well as one of the most influential preachers in Sudan, https://www.memri.org/reports/official-friday-sermons-sudan-our-son-obama-hussein-taking-same-path-his-predecessor-has, 27 August 2004, checked on 26 April 2017. See also video on http://www.memri.org/legacy/clip/224.

213 Official PA daily, Al-Hayat Al-Jadida, 27 July 2011, http://palwatch.org/main.aspx?fi=1031&all=1, checked on 26 April 2017.

29.

"Apartheid" and Boycott, Divestment, Sanctions (BDS)

- Arab and Muslim Antizionists frequently call the state of Israel and its control of the territories it occupied in 1967, an apartheid regime, comparing it to the government policy of racial discrimination formerly practiced in South Africa.[214]
- It has led to an international campaign of Boycott, Divestment and Sanctions (BDS).[215]

"This report [of the 18 Arab countries members of the UN Economic and Social Commission of Western Asia] concludes that Israel has established an apartheid regime that dominates the Palestinian people as a whole. Aware of the seriousness of this allegation, the authors of the report conclude that available evidence establishes beyond a reasonable doubt that Israel is guilty of policies and practices that constitute the crime of apartheid as legally defined in instruments of international law".[216]

"[Dr Fouad Moughrabi] discussed discrimination and racial segregation as it exists in Palestine and under South African apartheid. He noted that segregation in Palestine, aimed at eliminat-

---

214 See section Omissions of Facts and Misrepresentations on p. 126.
215 See section Boycott, Disinvestment and Sanctions (BDS) on pp. 123-124.
216 Economic and Social Commission for Western Asia (ESCWA), United Nations, *Israeli Practices towards the Palestinian People and the Question of Apartheid Palestine and the Israeli Occupation*, Issue No. 1, Beirut, 2017, Executive Summary, p.1. https://electronicintifada.net/sites/default/files/2017-03/un_apartheid_report_15_march_english_final_.pdf, checked on 26 April 2017. ESCWA has a membership of 18 Arab countries, https://www.unescwa.org/about-escwa/overview/member-states. The UN secretary General asked for the report to be withdrawn, http://www.reuters.com/article/us-un-israel-report-resignation-idUSKBN16O24X.

ing and excluding the Palestinian nation, is worse than what was carried out in South Africa, since the aim there [in South Africa] was not to get rid of the land's original inhabitants…the aim of the agreements signed by Palestinians and Israelis is to perpetuate [Israel's] expansionist and Judaizing policies in the area".[217]

"This national BDS conference [The Fourth National BDS Conference, 8 June 2013, Bethlehem] provided a distinguished platform for exchanging ideas among Palestinian youth and student activists, trade unionists, women activists, decision makers, intellectuals, academics, representatives of the private sector, and leading NGO networks. The conference aimed to promote and enable Palestinian society's effective development of sector-based BDS campaigns with clear strategies and leadership teams. Recognizing how Israel is increasingly seeking Palestinian and other Arab "fig-leaves" to cover up its intensifying occupation, colonization and apartheid, one of the main themes addressed was the economic, academic, cultural, youth and IT sector normalization with Israel and ways of confronting it".[218]

"We, civic and human rights organizations of Egypt, Jordan, Lebanon and Palestine, in mobilization for Palestinian Prisoners' Day this year, call for the boycott of the G4S company in the Arab World because of its involvement in Israeli occupation and oppression. G4S is a multinational company providing private security services. Among its services, G4S, through its Israeli subsidiary, Hashmira, provides equipment for Israeli occupation checkpoints and for settlements in the West Bank".[219]

217 Dr. Fouad Moughrabi, former head of the Department of International Relations and Political Psychology at the American University of Tennessee, at The Ibrahim Abu Lughod Institute of International Studies at Birzeit University, Al-Hayat Al-Jadida, 1 November 2013, https://www.palwatch.org/main.aspx?fi=606&doc_id=10355, checked on 26 April 2017.
218 https://bdsmovement.net/files/2013/06/Fourth-National-BDS-Conference-Report-ENG-18-Jun-2013.pdf, checked on 27 April 2017.
219 Statement of 16 April 2013, https://bdsmovement.net/news/organizations-egypt-jordan-lebanon-and-palestine-call-g4s-boycott, checked on 27

30.

Coalescences of Antizionist Ideologies

- An ideology that is seeking to transform the world and replace it with a new order, is in an existential struggle with other ideologies seeking likewise to bring about their alternative new order. However, when it comes to Zionism and Israel, competing ideologies have lowered their barricades and come together.
- In the words of Professor Robert Wistrich

    "The anti-Zionism of the 1960s and 70s has led to a monolithic consensus in which it has become difficult if not impossible to distinguish left from right…traditional ideological distinctions have lost their meaning. Anti-Zionism has become the great bazaar in which Soviet and Chinese Communists, Arab and Third World Marxists, Trotskyists, anarchists and Castroists along with feudal sheiks, conservative Islamic rulers, oil companies and capitalist interests in the West (not to speak of fascist fringe-groups) can find common ground in their hatred of the Jewish State".[220]

- Antizionist ideologies have colluded in three different ways to advance an Antizionist International :

    Means: Many Antizionists have found a common denominator as a means to achieve their goal, Boycott, Divestment and Sanction or BDS[221], thereby again transcending their conflicting ideologies.

April 2017.
220 Robert S.Wistrich, *Introduction* in *The Left Against Zion*, R.S. Wistrich ed., London, 1979, pp.Vlll-LX.
221 See pp. 123-124.

Borrowing ideological elements from each other: Many Antizionists have also frequently relied on ideological themes that are extrinsic and even antithetical to the particular ideology to which they subscribe. Right-wing conspiracy theories have found a fertile terrain amongst Muslim, Arab, Christian and Left-wing Antizionists. Muslim, Arab, Christian and Right-wing Antizionists attack Israel/Zionism as being "capitalist", "colonialist" and "imperialist" which is clearly left-wing in origin.[222]

Operating together: Finally, there is ample evidence of representatives of the various conflicting ideologies meeting at various forums to coordinate their Antizionist activities.[223]

---

222   Henri Stellman, *Christian Anti-Zionism,* in *The Wiener Library Bulletin,* 1981, vol. XXXlV, new series nos. 53/54, pp.34-35; Dave Rich, *The Left's Jewish Problem, Jeremy Corbyn, Israel and Anti-Semitism,* London, 2016. In 2012, Jeremy Corbyn, the leader of the British labour Party, defended a London mural which depicted Jewish bankers counting money around a board balanced on men with dark complexions, a typical Right-wing Antisemitic trope, *Haaretz,* 25 March 2018.
223   For example, in July 1976, an *International Symposium on Zionism and Racism,* was convened in Tripoli, Lybia, and was attended by 500 participants from 80 counties and included clergyman, socialists and Jews, *Zionism and Racism,* International Organization for the Elimination of All Forms of Racial Discrimination, Tripoli, n.d. Another similar conference took place in Bagdad in 1976, *Zionism, Imperialism and Racism,* A.W. Kayyli ed., London, 1979. Yet another similar conference took place in Tehran in 2014 https://cst.org.uk/news/blog/2014/10/02/rev-stephen-sizer-speaking-at-antisemitic-conference-in-iran checked on 1 November 2016.

Part 3

Is Antizionism Antisemitic?
Other Dimensions

31.

Violent Antizionism

Antizionism seems to cause manifestations of anti-Semitism, to encourage closet anti-Semites to come into the open and enables those who are already openly anti-Semitic to intensify their anti-Jewish hostility. There is considerable evidence of acts of violence having been committed over the years against Jews because of hatred of Zionism and Israel and the perceived position of the Jews in the Diaspora as supporting Zionism/Israel.[224]

- One of the worst atrocities took place in July 1994 when an explosive devise targeted the Jewish community building in Buenos Aires in the heart of a Jewish neighbourhood, an attack in which eighty-six people lost their lives and many more were wounded. The track of the terrorists led clearly to Iran, a fierce propagandist of Antizionist ideology.[225]
- On 19 March 2012, three children and a Rabbi were murdered in a Jewish school in Toulouse by Mohammad Merah, an Islamist jihadi who had said that he wanted to avenge the deaths of Palestinian children.[226]
- Ehdi Nemmouche, who had spent over a year in Syria and had links with radical Islamists, attacked the Jewish Museum in Brussels, killing 3 people, on 24 May 2014.[227]

---

224 The focus here is on violent acts. Antisemitic monitoring agencies have a wider brief and also include other incidents. For example, the *Community Security Trust* in Britain includes damage and desecration to Jewish property and threats, amongst others. See https://cst.org.uk/data/file/b/e/Incidents%20Report%202016.1486376547.pdf, checked on 28 April 2017.
225 Phyllis Chesler, *The New Anti-Semitism*, San Francisco, 2003, pp. 58-59.
226 https://www.thejc.com/news/world/funerals-of-toulouse-victims-as-suspect-surrounded-by-police-1.32401?highlight=Mohammad-Merah, checked on 28 April 2017.
227 http://www.bbc.co.uk/news/world-europe-27654505, checked on 28 April 2017.

- Four Jews were murdered in a Paris kosher supermarket by a Jihadist on 9 January 2015. The victims were killed after they were taken hostage by terrorist Amedy Coulibaly at the Hyper Cacher supermarket in eastern Paris.[228]

---

228 https://www.thejc.com/news/israel/victims-of-paris-supermarket-attack-buried-in-jerusalem-1.64544, checked on 28 April 2017.

32.

The Antisemitic Aspect of Boycotts

The boycott of Israel can be defined as a refusal to buy from, do business or collaborate with companies or organisations associated with the state of Israel as an expression of protest to the existence of the state or to its policies, or as a means to coerce Israel to alter its policies.

- In Palestine, during the decades preceding the establishment of the Jewish State in 1948, there were regular initiatives by the Arab population to boycott people, goods and businesses of the Jewish community, as a protest against the nascent Zionist nation-building. In his book *Terre Promise, Trop Promise- Genese du Conflict Israelo-Palestinien (1882-1948),* Nathan Weinstock gives numerous examples of boycotts directed against the local Jewish population. These were not only grassroots initiatives but also acts initiated by the leading organs of the Arab population. The Higher Arab Committee, which was created in 1936 and represented all the various nationalist Arabs of Palestine, actively promoted a boycott of the Jewish economic sector. When the Council of the Arab League was created, one of its first acts was to adopt a resolution on the 2nd of December 1945 which established a boycott of products originating from the Jewish sector. This was done with a view to isolating economically the Jewish community and rejecting from Arab countries goods developed by Jews in Palestine.[229]
- After the establishment of the State of Israel, the Arab nations have developed a campaign, through their Boycott Office, to blockade world trade with Israel. The targets are not only Israeli companies and other companies trading with Israel. According to Terrence Prittie and Walter Nelson, author of *The Economic War*

---

[229] Nathan Weinstock, *Terre Promise, Trop Promise - Genese du Conflict Israelo-Palestinien (1882-1948)*, Paris, 2011, pp.251,318 -319.

against the Jews, this means "discrimination against Jewish owned firms and [...] boycott pressure against the employment of Jews in non-Jewish firms. The most flagrant example in the 1960's was the Norwich Union affair, which involved the resignation of a Jewish peer, Lord Mancroft, from a British insurance company's board of directors, because of direct Arab pressure". Jewish banks such as Warburg, Lazard and Rothschild have also been blacklisted.[230]

- In 1975, the General Assembly of the United Nations passed a resolution that equated Zionism with Racism. Some pro-Palestinian campaigners at British universities linked the UN resolution to the "No Platform" for Racism policy that was passed a year later by the British National Union of Students. It, therefore, reached the conclusion that Zionism should be banned from student unions. As most Jewish students were Zionists and the only campus organisations promoting Zionism were the Jewish societies, this led to the expulsion of Jewish societies in several universities.[231]
- Following the 2014 military operation by Israel in Gaza, a branch of the Sainsbury supermarket chain in London pulled all kosher products from it shelves, following anti-Israel protests.[232]
- Also, following Israel's military operation, the Tricycle Theatre in London decided to stop hosting the UK Jewish Film Festival because of a small sponsorship from the Israeli Embassy.[233]
- In August 2015, a well-known American-Jewish singer Matisyahu was barred from an international music festival near Valencia in Spain after he refused to accede to the organisers' demands that he clarify his position to Zionism and the Israel-Palestine conflict.[234]

---

230 Terrence Prittie and Walter Nelson, *The Economic War against the Jews*, London, 1979, pp.69, 114.
231 Dave Rich, *Hatred at the Heart of the Campus War*, The Jewish Chronicle, 2 November 2015, http://www.thejc.com/comment-and-debate/comment/148444/hatred-heart-campus-wars, checked on 1 November 2016.
232 http://www.thetimes.co.uk/tto/news/uk/article4179551.ece, checked on 14 October 2014.
233 http://www.thetimes.co.uk/tto/opinion/thunderer/article4168823.ece, checked on 14 October 2014.
234 https://cst.org.uk/news/blog/2015/08/19/bds-and-morality-testing-for-

33.

Acknowledgement by Antizionists of Antisemitism

Some Antizionists openly declare that Antizionism is or can be Antisemitic.

- In March 2003, the Director of the *ArtMalaga* gallery in Spain refused to stage an exhibit by an Israeli artist Patricia Sassoon because, in his words, "we certainly hold an anti-Semitic attitude to any person related to that country". [235]
- Mahatir Mohammed, former Malaysian Prime Minister, wrote after an Israeli court in 2012 decided that the Israel Defence Forces had not been to blame for the death of a pro-Palestinian activist, that "I am glad to be labelled anti-Semitic. How can I be otherwise when the Jews who so often talk of the horrors they suffered during the Holocaust show the same Nazi cruelty and hard-heartedness towards not just their enemies but even towards their allies should any try to stop the senseless killing of their Palestinian enemies". [236]
- Even leading lights of BDS admit that their movement has sometimes succumbed to Antisemitism. American professor Judith Butler, BDS's premier philosopher and political theorist has acknowledged that some criticisms of Israel "do employ anti-Semitic rhetoric and argument". [237]

---

jews, checked om 27 April 2017. After widespread criticism, the boycott was subsequently reversed.

235 Amnon Rubinstein, *The Cheshire Smile of Anti-Semitism*, *Haaretz*, 11 March 2003, in Phyllis Chesler, op. cit. p.133.

236 http://chedet.cc/?p=837#, checked on 16 January 2018.

237 Judith Butler, *Parting ways: Jewishness and the Critique of Zionism*, New York, 2012, p. 116, in *The Case Against Academic Boycotts of Israel*, op.cit., p.251. Prof Butler adds that this rhetoric must be opposed absolutely and unequivocally; Cary Nelson, *The Problem with Judith Butler: The Politi-*

- The Scottish Parliament's Cross Party Group on Palestine has condemned as potentially Antisemitic the conduct of its own treasurer who refused to debate Antisemitism with representatives of various Zionist organisations, calling them "ideological terrorists".[238]
- Various prominent members of the British Labour Party have acknowledged that numerous party activists have expressed Antisemitic views and its leader Jeremy Corbyn has repeatedly apologised for his behaviour.[239]

---

     cal Philosophy of BDS and the movement to Delegitimate Israel, in *The Case Against Academic Boycotts of Israel*, op.cit., p.165.

238 25 April 2017, *Scottish MSP condemns 'astonishing' refusal to debate with Israel supporters,* http://jewishnews.timesofisrael.com/scottish-msp-condemns-astonishing-refusal-to-debate-with-israel-supporters/, checked on 11 May 2017.

239 See for example Hirsh, op.cit., and *The Jewish Chronicle* of 24 April and 2 August 2018

34.

Zionism as a Code Word

- Zionism is used as a code word for Judaism. Antizionists often use the word "Zionists" or, alternatively "Zio", a term used by far-right anti-Semitic groups, when they refer to members of the diaspora Jewish community as a way to cover up an Antisemitic statement.
- In 1969, Dr Hafez Ismael, the ex-Ambassador of the United Arab Republic to France said that as long as Israel will be a nation supported by "12 million Zionists" from all over the world, there would be something foreign in that part of the world. As there were approximately 12 million Jews outside Israel at the time, it is quite clear that by "12 million Zionists", Ambassador Ismael meant 12 million Jews. Since he was afraid that accusing the Jews of the world will create bad publicity, he substituted the word "Zionists" for "Jews".[240]
- The president of the British National Union of Students, David Aaronovitch, now a well-known journalist, was the victim of a campaign of forged letters in 1981 which alleged that he was in the pay of the Israeli Embassy in London. The British Antizionist Organisation (BAZO) which published these letters claimed that Aaronovitch has a "Zionist" name. There is of course no such thing as a Zionist name, only a Jewish sounding name.[241]
- In 1972, the Soviet Embassy in Paris was charged with circulating Antisemitic literature in one of its publications. The Soviet Embassy used as its defence the argument that the article in question was directed at "Zionists", not Jews. Grigory Svirsky,

---

[240] Press conference on 12 August 1969 to the French Press Association, *Le Monde*, 15 August 1969.
[241] *Jewish Observer*, vol. 38, no 2, February 1981, in *The Jerusalem Post International Edition*, 22-28 February 1981.

an expert in Russian Antisemitism, produced for the Paris tribunal quotations from an Antisemitic publication of the infamous Cossack band, the Black Hundreds. The two texts, that of the Soviet Embassy publication and that of the Black Hundreds were identical but for one small but significant detail – in the Soviet Embassy's publication each mention of the word "Jew" had been replaced by the word "Zionist". The Paris tribunal found the Embassy guilty and fined it heavily.[242]
- In a message sent on Facebook, Rayhan Uddin who had been running for the post of general secretary of the *London School of Economics Student Union* in March 2016, asserted that *"*leading Zionists*"* had attempted to "win back the LSE and make it right wing and Zio again*".*[243]
- Khadim Hussain, a former Lord Mayor of Bradford, was suspended from Labour after he shared a Facebook post tha*t referred to* "the six million Zionists that were killed by Hitler".[244]
- Nazim Ali, director of the Islamic Human Rights Commission, organizer of the annual Al Quds Antizionist demonstration in London, said through a public-address system as he led the march on 18 June 2017:

> "We are fed up of the Zionists, we are fed up with all their rabbis; we are fed up with all their synagogues, we are fed up with their supporters. As we know in Grenfell [a high-rise tower in London where many of its tenants perished as the result of a fire] many innocents were murdered by Theresa May's cronies, many of which are supporters of Zionist ideology. Let us not forget that some of the biggest corporations who were supporting the Conservative Party are Zionists. They are responsible for the murder of the people of Grenfell, in those towers in Grenfell, the Zionist supporters

---

242 Arnold Ages, *Anti-Semitism versus Anti-Zionism, Conservative Judaism*, vol. 31, no 4, Summer 1972. See also Emanual Litvinoff, *Soviet Anti-Semitism: The Paris Trial*, London, 1974.
243 http://www.thejc.com/node/154476, checked on 1 November 2016.
244 http://www.bbc.co.uk/news/magazine-36160928, checked on 1 November 2016.

of the Tory Party. It is the Zionists who give money to the Tory party, to kill people in high-rise blocks. Free Free Palestine".[245]

---

245 *The Jewish Chronicle*, 23 June 2017.

35.

Antizionism as Double-Standard

Here Zionism and the State of Israel are judged according to one measure, the Arab countries and other parties according to another. What makes this form of Antizionism Antisemitic is that it is the Jews, as such, who are the target of the particular form of attack.

- The concept of self-determination as applied by Antizionists is a good illustration of this point. The principle of self-determination is defined as the right of people to decide their own political future. According to Antizionists, it is up to each people to decide whether it forms such an entity, entitling it to the right of self-determination. The Palestinians, it is claimed, consider themselves a people, and as such have the right to demand a state of their own. Yet the Jews, who also consider themselves a people, are denied that same right. The Antizionists who use this double standard, take it upon themselves to decide that no matter how the Jews regard themselves, they do not form a people and are therefore not entitled to a state of their own. The subjective standard of self-determination is transformed in the case of the Jews into quite a different standard.[246]
- Antizionists often criticize Jews of the world for supporting Israel. The criticism often does not refer to the *substance* of Jewish support for Israel but rather to the *act* of supporting it. It is said that in supporting Israel, or its policies, or Zionism, Jews living in other countries over-step their rights as citizens of the coun-

---

246 *Seminar of Arab Jurists on Palestine, Algiers, 22-27 July 1967 – The Palestine Question*, Institute For Palestine Studies, Beirut, 1968; Lahav Harkov, *Arab MK Zoabi – Jews Not Entitled To Self-determination, The Jerusalem Post,* 13 October 2017, www.lpost/Israel-News/Arab-MK-Zoabi-not-entitled-to-self-determination-507309, checked on 11 January 2018.

tries in which they live. In more extreme variations, Jews are accused of "dual loyalty", i.e. the absurd view that support for the country of which one is a citizen and support for Israel cannot be reconciled. Israel's opponents will, of course, see nothing wrong in the Palestinians who live as citizens in different counties of the world, or for that matter, the millions of Arabs scattered across so many nations, supporting the establishment of a Palestinian state.[247]

---

247 John J. Mearsheimer and Stephen M. Walt, *The Israel Lobby and U.S. Foreign Policy*, London, 2007; Adam Kredo, *White House, Allies Accuse Jewish Lawmakers of Dual Loyalty To Israel*, http://freebeacon.com/national-security/white-house-allies-accuse-jewish-lawmakers-of-dual-loyalty-to-israel/, checked on 16 January 2018. See also the accusation levelled at the journalist Melanie Phillips on the BBC TV panel show "Question Time", *The Times*, 19 June 2018.

36.

The Consequences of Antizionism

The substance of this theory is that since support for Zionism and the existence State of Israel is shared by an overwhelming majority of Jews around the world and since Israel is seen as an important, if not central dimension of Jewish identity, it follows that an attack on the State of Israel is, therefore an attack on Jews all over the world.

- For Professor Shlomo Avineri of the Hebrew University of Jerusalem, it is a fact that most Jews today define themselves in some way or another, and in various degrees of intensity, in relation to Israel. Should Israel disappear, or a major catastrophe befalls it, practically all Jewish people would conceive it as a major tragedy for their own existence as Jews. Therefore, a deligitimization of Israel is tantamount to the deligitimization of Jewish existence as understood today by most Jews.[248]
- For Professor Kenneth L. Marcus of Brandeis University

   "certain forms of hostility towards Israel are anti-Semitic in the sense that they cause foreseeable harm to Jews based on a trait that is central to Jewish identity […] Some abuse of Israel by the BDS campaign is profoundly offensive to Jews because of the intimate relationship between a person's Jewish identity and that person attachment to Israel. Indeed, for many Jews, a commitment to Israel is so intrinsic to their religious belief as to be the paradigmatic case of a characteristic that a people should not be required to change. For those Jews who embrace Israel as part of their Jewish identity, the commitment may be of multi-generational duration, shared

---

248   Shlomo Avineri, *Anti-Semitism Today: A Symposium, Patterns of Prejudice*, vol.16, no 4, October 1982, pp.4-5.

historically by many members of the group, inscribed centrally in the group's common literature and tradition, and pervasive of the culture".[249]

- This is not an absurd claim by any means, writes Jonathan Freedland, from *The Guardian*.

  "Jewish affinity with Israel is now so widespread and entrenched, across the political and religious spectrum, that it has indeed become a central part of Jewish identity [...] This should give the anti-Zionist pause; much as they may insist that they condemn only Zionists, not Jews, this is not how Jews themselves experience it. The Jewish people has made up its mind since 1945 and it has embraced Zionism. To stand against that idea now is to stand against a core Jewish belief".[250]

- If we look at the main themes of Antizionism for the last few decades, we note in particular the equating of Zionism with Nazism. Since most Jews identify closely with Israel, an anti-Jewish dimension can be seen in this charge. In other words, accusing Zionism and Israel of Nazism is tantamount to accusing the Jews of the world of being Nazis, a rather cynical inversion of yesterday's victim into today's perpetrators.

---

249 Kenneth L. Marcus, Is *the Boycott, Divestment, and Sanctions Movement Anti-Semitic?*, in *The Case Against Academic Boycotts of Israel*, op.cit. p.252.
250 Jonathan Freedland, *Is Anti-Zionism Antisemitism?*, in *A New Antisemitism? Debating Judeophobia in 21st-Century Britain*, ed. by Paul Iganski and Barry Kosmin, London, 2003, p.122.

37.

Fellow Antizionist Travellers

The concept of Antizionists colluding with anti-Semites without being themselves anti-Semitic – originally developed in the context of the Bolshevik revolution – has been analysed by Anthony Julius:

- "They are often found defending anti-Semites –not guilty of the offense themselves, but quick to champion others who are guilty of it… They share space with anti-Semites, untroubled by the company they keep; they comprise a species of 'fellow traveller'… the kind of person ready to overlook or excuse everything that is vicious in the cause he supports, the protagonists he admires".[251]
- In March 2009, the well- known British film director Ken Loach responded to a report on the growth of Antisemitism since the beginning of the Gaza War. Loach described the report as "a red herring", adding that "[i]f there has been a rise I am not surprised. In fact, it is perfectly understandable because Israel feeds feelings of anti-Semitism." [252]
- Jean Bauberot, a past leader of the French Christian Students Association wrote that to be against all forms of racism is as stupid as being against all forms of violence; that Palestinians have the right to appear anti-Semitic to *'us'*. [Bouberot then moves away from the position of an outside colluder when he writes that to demonstrate the intricacies of the Palestine problem forces *'us'* to treat the Jews as oppressors and that *'we'* are allowed to use identical terms and parts of sentences used by Hitler even if we have nothing in common with that ideology].[253]

---

251 Anthony Julius, *Trials of the Diaspora – A History of Anti-Semitism in England*, Oxford, 2010, p. 522.
252 *EU-wide rise in anti-Semitism described as 'understandable', EU Politics News*, 4 March 2009.
253 Jean Bauberot, *La Vie de l'Alliance, Herytem*, May-July 1969.

38.

Separate Antisemitic and Antizionist Views in Same Individuals

Researchers were interested to see whether a proponent of extreme anti-Israel views also holding simultaneously separate anti-Semitic views, was a prevalent occurrence. Professors Edward Kaplan and Charles Small arrived at the conclusion that there was a correlation between the two:

- "In the discourse surrounding the Israeli-Palestinian conflict, extreme criticisms of Israel (e.g., Israel is an apartheid state, the Israel Defence Forces deliberately target Palestinian civilians), coupled with extreme policy proposals (e.g., boycott of Israeli academics and institutions, divest from companies doing business with Israel), have sparked counterclaims that such criticisms are anti-Semitic (for only Israel is singled out). The research in this article shines a different, statistical light on this question: based on a survey of 500 citizens in each of 10 European countries, the authors ask whether those individuals with extreme anti-Israel views are more likely to be anti-Semitic. Even after controlling for numerous potentially confounding factors, they find that anti-Israel sentiment consistently predicts the probability that an individual is anti-Semitic, with the likelihood of measured anti-Semitism increasing with the extent of anti-Israel sentiment observed." [254]

---

254 Edward H Kaplan and Charles A Small, *Anti-Israel Sentiment Predicts Anti-Semitism in Europe,* Abstract, *The Journal of Conflict Resolution,* August 2006, vol. 50, no. 4, pp. 548-561. L Daniel Staetsky, *Antisemitism in contemporary Great Britain - A study of attitudes towards Jews and Israel,* JPR Report, September 2017.

- Jackie Walker, a British left-wing Jewish Antizionist, has expressed Antisemitic views distinct from her Antizionist views. She wrote on her Facebook that Jews were the "chief financiers of the sugar and slave trade".[255]

---

[255] *Jewish Chronicle,* 2 June and 7 October 2016; *The Times,* 5 October 2016; Dave Rich, op.cit., pp. 242-246.

39.

Unintentional Antisemitism in Antizionism

According to British academic Dr David Hirsh, it is now widely accepted among antiracist scholars and activists that "acts, speeches, ideas, practices, or institutions may be racist or may lead to racist outcomes, independently of whether or not the people involved are judged to be self-consciously racist".[256]

The report by Lord Scarman on the 1981 London Brixton riots, repeated and expanded by the British Judge Macpherson in 1999 in his enquiry on the Stephen Lawrence murder, accepted the existence of "unwitting", "unconscious" and "unintentional" racism.[257]

- On 14 January 2002, the *New Statesman* weekly published on its front cover a star of David piercing a union jack flag with the headline "A Kosher Conspiracy". The issue featured two articles analysing the influence of the pro-Israel lobby. The editor of the New Statesman, Peter Wilby, wrote subsequently "We (or more precisely, I) got it wrong" and that "The cover was not intended to be anti-Semitic, the *New Statesman* is vigorously opposed to racism in all its forms. But it used images and words in such a way as to create unwittingly the impression that the New Statesman was following an anti-Semitic tradition that sees the Jews as a conspiracy piercing the heart of the nation."[258]

---

256 David Hirsh, *Hostility to Israel and Antisemitism: Toward a Sociological Approach, Journal for the Study of Antisemitism,* JSA Vol 5#1, 2013, p.1413.
257 Macpherson William, *Report of the Stephen Lawrence Inquiry*, February 24, 1999, http://www.archive.official documents.co.uk/document/cm42/4262/sli-06.htm, checked on 25 April 2014.
258 *New Statesman*, 11 February 2002.

- In a message sent on Facebook, Rayhan Uddin who had been running for the post of general secretary of the London School of Economics Student Union, asserted that "leading Zionists" had attempted to "win back the LSE and make it right wing and Zio again". In a subsequent message on Facebook, he apologised as follows: "it is utterly repugnant to me to think that I may have unwittingly appeared to endorse in any way the foul ideology of antisemitism".[259]

---

259 http://www.thejc.com/node/154476, checked on 1 November 2016.

Part 4

The Means of Antizionism

40.

Violence

- Violence has been a means used frequently by Antizionists to achieve their goal.
- Amongst violent tactics used by Antizionists are wars, uprisings, hostage takings, plane hijackings, stones being thrown, stabbings, shootings, bombings and arson attacks.
- In terms of casualties, it has been estimated that in Palestine/Israel, thousands of Israelis/Jews have been killed or wounded as a result of terrorism and other violence.[260]

---

260   https://www.jewishvirtuallibrary.org/total-casualties-arab-israeli-conflict, checked on 9 February 2017.

41.

Cartoons

- Antizionists frequently use drawings to express their views on Zionism/Israel.

As you get ready to celebrate Halloween today, please spare a thought for Palestine, where every day and every night is full of horror and terror at the hands of the Israeli occupation forces.

Horror Costumes[261]

---

261 Excerpt from Facebook Page Entry: "*Ireland Palestine Solidarity Campaign, October 31, 2015,*" *Ireland Palestine Solidarity Campaign*, Accredited by the *UN Committee on the Exercise of the Inalienable Rights of the Palestinian People,* http://www.humanrightsvoices.org/assets/images/panels/list_10/Report-on-UN-NGOs-Spreading-Antisemitism-Terror-September-2016.pdf, checked on 11 May 2017.

The Final Solution[262]

---

262 Cartoon of Israeli Prime Minister Menachem Begin in Britain's *Labour Herald*, 25 June 1982, http://www.haaretz.com/opinion/1.781902, checked on 11 May 2017.

Happy Mothers' Day Palestine[263]

---

263 Official Fatah Facebook page, 21 March 2107, cartoon by Carlos Latuff, http://www.palwatch.org/site/modules/cartoons/cartoons.aspx?fld_id=latest&doc_id=20827, Palwatch has added their logo on the cartoon, checked on 11 May 2017.

42.

Boycott, Divestment and Sanction (BDS)

- In 2001, a United Nations conference in Durban, South Africa was convened to deal with the global fight against racism. At an associated meeting of Non-Governmental Organisations, the following resolution was adopted:

  "NGO Declaration, World Conference against Racism, Racial Discrimination, Xenophobia and Related Intolerance, Durban, September 2001: Call for… adoption of all measures… employed against the South African Apartheid regime (Article 418) Call for the launch of an international anti-Israeli Apartheid movement as implemented against South African Apartheid through a global solidarity campaign network of international civil society (Article 424) Impose a policy of complete and total isolation of Israel as an apartheid state…the imposition of mandatory and comprehensive sanctions and embargoes, the full cessation of all links (diplomatic, economic, social, aid, military cooperation and training) between all states and Israel (Article 425)".[264]

- In 2005, an alliance of 170 Palestinian organizations in Israel, the Palestine Authority and overseas came together as a coalition entitled "The Palestinian Civil Society Calls for Boycott, Divestment and Sanctions [BDS] Against Israel".[265]

---

264 *Boycott, Disinvestment, Sanctions*, http://honestreporting.com/wp-content/uploads/2012/07/BDS-an-Introduction.pdf checked on 24 February 2015. For a definition, see pp. 21 and 22 above.
265 Ibid.

- Boycotts and the BDS campaign have subsequently spread around the world to college campuses, churches, trade unions and other arenas. It has become the lynchpin of the Antizionist movement around the world, often expressed as a rallying cry in its discourse and activities.

43.

Omissions of Facts and Misrepresentation

- Spoken or written accounts of events are by universal consensus subject to standards of accuracy, impartiality and fairness. Often Antizionists are guilty of violating these benchmarks. Amongst the types of bias that can be found are omissions of facts and misrepresentations.
- Example: The claim that the United Nations issued the Right of Return of all Palestinian refugees.[266]

> The claim that the resolution grants all the refugees an absolute right of repatriation is misleading. Resolution 194 of the General Assembly of December 1948, does not mention a Right of Return. Article 11 of the resolution is restricted to refugees wishing to return to their homes "and live at peace with their neighbours" who "should be permitted to do so at the earliest practicable date" because it was obvious to the UN that the return of a hostile fifth column could endanger the existence of Israel. Furthermore, as the resolution was passed by the General Assembly of the UN, it is not legally binding according to its charter, a fact highlighted by the use of the word "should" in the resolution. Last but not least, Arab states rejected the resolution.[267]

---

266 See for example www.1948.org.uk/right-of-return/ chequed on 13 January 2018; https://www.palwatch.org/main.aspx?fi=790&doc_id=19751, checked on 25 April 2017.

267 https://www.jewishvirtuallibrary.org/jsource/myths3/MFrefugees.html#9, checked on 1 February 2017.

- Example: The claim that Israel's treatment of Arab Israeli citizens within Israel's pre-1967 border, is similar to the treatment of black people in apartheid South Africa.[268]

    The fallacy of the claim lies in its selection of certain unrepresentative similarity features between Israel and apartheid South Africa whilst omitting the significant differences between the two (unlike apartheid South Africa, Arab Israelis enjoy citizenship and equal rights, are able to vote and serve in the Israeli parliament, serve in the cabinet, in high-level foreign ministry positions, in the judiciary including the Supreme Court;
    they enjoy the freedom of movement, assembly and speech; schools, universities and hospitals make no distinction between Arab and Jews; Jews and Arabs share meals in restaurants and travel together on trains, buses and taxis).[269] Moreover, those Antizionists who accuse Israel also ignore considerable evidence pointing to the fact that the analogy with apartheid is more appropriate for Arab countries, many of them are dictatorial regimes with appalling human rights records when it comes to the treatment of groups such as Christians, Jews, Kurds, political dissidents, women and homosexuals.[270]

- Example: The accusation of colonialism and imperialism levelled at Zionism/Israel.[271]

Here one is hard pressed to find any similarity between Zionism and Colonialism:

- The Zionists were never the agent settlers of any mother country for whose economic or political benefit they exploited the native population;

---

268   See for example pp. 92-99 above.
269   http://www.bicom.org.uk/analysis/20001/, checked on 1 February 2017.
270   http://www.jewishvirtuallibrary.org/myths-and-facts-human-rights-in-arab-countries, checked on 26 April 2017.
271   See for example Left Antizionism pp. 27-50 and section entitled Colonialism/Imperialism in Arab/Muslim Antizionism on pp. 90 and 91.

- A typical feature of colonialism is the lack of historical connection between the colonial parent state and its representative settlers with the lands they were settling. Zionism, on the other hand, represented a return of the Jews to their historic homeland to reclaim the land of their ancestors;
- Furthermore, how does the colonial model of symbiosis between the parent state and the settlers fit in with the increasingly ferocious attacks by the Zionist immigrants on the British forces during the Mandate?
- Moreover, the Zionists did not steal land and did not systematically expel the inhabitants, they purchased the land legally.
- The Zionist movement was permeated with a strong dose of socialism, the antithesis of capitalism.[272]

Facing the Zionists on the other side, the Arab world was showing the characteristics of a feudal, reactionary society:

- Most Arab states were themselves created by the imperialist powers of Great Britain and France and continue to receive significant support after the establishment of Israel from the Soviet Union and others.
- Last but not east, the Arab nation has expanded with the sword into a vast empire in the past, reaching as far as France, Austria, Italy and Hungary. It is worth recalling Jordan's occupation of the West Bank in 1948, a territory meant to be allocated by the UN to an independent Palestinian state, along with Syria's occupation of Lebanon and Saddam Hussein invasion of Kuwait. Israel's occupation of the West Bank in 1967, on the other hand, was unpremeditated and in self-defence.[273]

---

[272] Nathan Weinstock, *Histoire de Chiens*, n.p., 2004, pp. 97-108; Nathan Weinstock, *Terre Promise, Trop Promise, Genese du Conflit Israelo-Palestinien (1882-1948)*, Paris, p.58.

[273] Efraim Karsh, *Islamic Imperialism, A History*, London, 2006.

44.

Falsifications

- Spoken or written accounts of events are by universal consensus subject to standards of accuracy, impartiality and fairness. Often Antizionists are guilty of violating these benchmarks. Amongst the types of bias that can be found are falsifications. Sometimes enemies of Zionism/Israel deliberately doctor facts in order to portray the country in a bad or worse light, for example through the manipulation of pictures.
- Example: In 2016, a Reuters photograph of smoke rising from buildings in Beirut had been withdrawn by the news agency after it was claimed that the photograph was doctored to include more smoke and damage. The photograph showed two very heavy plumes of black smoke billowing from buildings in Beirut after an Israeli Air Force attack on the Lebanese capital. Reuters subsequently withdrew the photograph from its website, publishing a message admitting that the image was distorted and offering an apology.[274]
- Example: A photo that was tweeted allegedly depicting the results of Israeli air strikes in Gaza in 2012, was proven false. The photo allegedly depicting a Palestinian girl killed by an Israeli air strike, was proven to have originated in 2006 and to have had nothing at all to do with Israeli action.[275]

---

274 http://www.ynetnews.com/articles/0,7340,L-3286966,00.html, checked on 1 February 2017.
275 https://www.idfblog.com/2012/03/12/photos-gaza-aerial-strikes-proven-false/, checked on 1 February 2017.

45.

Decontextualization

- Spoken or written accounts of events are by universal consensus subject to standards of accuracy, impartiality and fairness. Often Antizionists are guilty of violating these benchmarks. Amongst the types of bias that can be found are decontextualization. An awareness of context is essential for those examining, assessing and judging a country's behaviour. Critics of Israel often see it as acting in a vacuum. They fail to see or refuse to consider external events that explain why Israel has acted or not acted in a certain way.
- Example: The condemnation of Israel's blockade of Gaza without any explanation for the reasons for Israel's action.

> On September 7, 2016, *The Guardian* published the following story: "The Palestinian fishing industry operates under strictly enforced restrictions. An exclusion zone policed by Israel limits the industry's range to within six miles off Gaza's coast. Fishermen risk being shot at, arrested and having their catch confiscated." However, it failed to mention why Israel has implemented a maritime exclusion zone: the smuggling of weapons by Hamas.[276]

---

[276] http://honestreporting.com/the-guardian-filleting-the-context/, http://honestreporting.com/reuters-throws-vital-context-overboard/, checked on 1 February 2017.

46.

Exaggerations

- Spoken or written accounts of events are by universal consensus subject to standards of accuracy, impartiality and fairness. Often Antizionists are guilty of violating these benchmarks. Amongst the types of bias that can be found are exaggerations. Sometimes events are being represented considerably worse than the reality.
- Example: The false accusation that Israel committed a massacre in the Jenin refugee camp in April 2002.

> In April 2002, the Palestinian Authority made baseless accusations that Israeli forces has "massacred" Palestinian civilians in the Jenin refugee camp in April 2002. Incontrovertible evidence subsequently proved that no such massacre had occurred.[277]

---

277 http://www.jewishvirtuallibrary.org/myths-and-facts-the-palestinian-uprisings#q1, http://www.jewishvirtuallibrary.org/jsource/UN/jenin.html, checked on 1 February 2017.

47.

Double Standards

- Spoken or written accounts of events are by universal consensus subject to standards of accuracy, impartiality and fairness. Often Antizionists are guilty of violating these benchmarks. Amongst the types of bias that can be found are double standards. With this technique, Zionism/Israel are judged according to one measure, the Arab countries and other parties, according to another.
- Example: The regular condemnation of Israel by the United Nations General Assembly and the UN Human Rights Council while the behaviour of repressive regimes are largely ignored. Contrary to the equality guarantee of the UN Charter, the UN General Assembly continues to single out Israel by 20 one-sided resolutions each year in the General Assembly—when the entire rest of the world combined receives 4 resolutions. Likewise, at the UN's Human Rights Council, Israel is the only country in the world to be targeted under a special agenda item—at every meeting. The Secretary General has condemned this. The council keeps a permanent investigator into "Israel's violations." At the same time, the real human rights violators instead get elected to high positions to the UN Human Rights Council.[278]

---

278   http://www.unwatch.org/en/, checked on 1 February 2017.

48.

The Spheres of Antizionism

- The campaign against Zionism and the State of Israel has encompassed many facets of domestic society and the international arena. These are the main areas where it has been most active: Academia, Campus, Websites, Social Media, Television, Radio, Newspapers, Arts, Culture, Sports, Labour Unions, Religions, Politics, International Institutions, Law, Schools, Architecture, Medicine and Entertainment.
- Example: Labour Unions in various countries have been active in the campaign against Zionism/Israel. Several trade unions have espoused a narrative siding unequivocally with the enemies of the Jewish State. In the UK, for example

  "the Trades Union Congress (TUC) and member unions have regularly adopted resolutions containing anti-Israeli and pro-Palestinian rhetoric. A whole generation of British left-wing trade union activists has been raised on a diet of conference motions whose only mention of Israel is in connection with its 'brutality' and 'oppression' of the Palestinian people".[279]

Various British unions have adopted the Boycott, Divestment and Sanction (BDS) campaign and cooperated with the leading British Antizionist organisation, the Palestine Solidarity Campaign (PSC). The anti-Israeli activism of one British union, the University Lecturers Union (UCU) led many of its Jewish members to resign their membership.[280]

---

279   Ronnie Fraser, *The British Trade Movement, Israel and Boycotts*, http://jcpa.org/article/the-british-trade-union-movement-israel-and-boycotts/, checked on 10 February 2017.

280   Ibid. See also *Dreams Deferred: A Concise Guide to the Israeli-Palestinian Conflict and the Movement to Boycott Israel*, ed. By Cary Nelson, Bloomington, 2016, pp.72-77.

Part 5

Tools for Activists and Analysts

49.

A short list of resources

- **Monitoring**

https://www.memri.org/
https://www.palwatch.org/
http://www.jpost.com/
http://www.timesofisrael.com/

- **Analysis**

The Case Against Academic Boycotts of Israel, ed. by Cary Nelson and Gabriel Noah Brahm, Chicago, 2015.
Deciphering the New Antisemitism, ed. by Alvin H Rosenfeld, Bloomington, 2015.
Dreams Deferred: A Concise Guide to the Israeli-Palestinian Conflict and the Movement to Boycott Israel, ed. by Cary Nelson, Bloomington, 2016.

- **Refutation**

http://www.jewishvirtuallibrary.org/
http://honestreporting.com/
http://www.camera.org/
http://mfa.gov.il/MFA/PressRoom/Pages/MFA-Spokesperson.aspx
Tom S van Bemmelen*, 150 Palestinian tales: Facts to better understand the Arab-Israeli Conflict,* Soesterberg ,2016.

50.

Revision Questions

Part 1: The Foundation

1. Definition of Antizionism
What is Antizionism?
What is Politicidal Antizionism?
What is Anti-Israel Antizionism?
What is Delegitimization?
What is Dehumanisation?
What is Demonization?
What is the difference between Antizionism and criticism of Israel's policies?

2. Definition of Related Concepts
What is Antisemitism according to the International Holocaust Remembrance Alliance (IHRA)?
What does the IHRA definition say about Israel?
What is the Boycott, Divestment and Sanction campaign?
What is the Boycott of Israel?
What is the Divestment from Israel?
What are Sanctions with regards to Israel?
What is Differentiation?
What is Intersectionality?
What is Lawfare?
What is Pink-washing?

3. The Motives of Antizionism
What could the motives of Antizionism be?
What could geo-political and commercial motives be?
What could psychological motives be?
What could politically correct motives be?

Part 2: Is Antizionism Antisemitic? The Ideological Dimension

Left Antizionism
What is Left Antizionist ideology?
Why does the interest of the ideologues of the Left in the "Jewish Question" come as no surprise?
Why does the opposition of scores of people of the Left to Israel and support of a campaign of delegitimization come as a surprise?
What can one say about Karl Marx with regards to Zionism?
What did Marx write about the Jews?
What is self-hatred?

4. Karl Kaustky
Why are Kautsky's views on Zionism so important?
What were his views on how to solve the Jewish problem?
Why did he consider Zionism as reactionary?
Why did he consider Zionism as racist?
What did he write about the meeting of Herzl with Plehve?
What was Kautsky's analysis of Zionism within the Palestinian context?
What was Kautsky's view on British colonialism in Palestine?
What was Kautsky's view on the relation between the Jewish settlers and the local Arab population?

5. The Bund
What was the view of Bundists on Jewish values and identity?
What was Autonomism?
What was the Bundist view that Zionism was against Socialism?
What was the Bundist view on the situation in Palestine?
What was the view of the Bund on the Balfour Declaration?
What was Vladimir Medem's view on Zionism?
What was Emanuel Scherer's view on Zionism?
What was Liebmann Hersh's view on Zionism?

6. Eduard Bernstein
What was Eduard Bernstein's view on Zionism?

7. Lenin
What were the two categories in which Lenin divided the Jews?
What did Lenin understand by his categorisation of Jews as a 'caste'?
What solution did Lenin advocate for the Jews?
What did Lenin write about anyone resisting assimilation?

8. Trotsky
What did Trotsky write about Herzl?
What was Trotsky's view on British policies in Palestine?

9. After 1917
Why did Left Antizionism become so important after 1917?
How did the new Russian leaders see the international scene?
How did the new Russian leaders see Zionism in their domestic environment?
What was the Soviet Union's position on Zionism after the Second World War?

10. Communist Parties in Non-Communist Countries
What was the view of the Palestine Communist Party on Zionism?
What was the view of the American Communist Party on Zionism?

11. After the Independence of Israel
What was the view of the Soviet Union after Israel's independence?
What is the significance of the book *Judaism without Embellishment*?
What was the Soviet's reaction to the 1967 Six-Day war?

12. Contemporary Themes
What was Abraham Leon's view on Zionism?
What are Lenni Brenner's and Ken Livingstone's views on the relationship between Nazism and Zionism?

Conspiracy Antizionism
What is the conspiracy theory?

13. Christian

What was *Civilta Cattolica's* view on the creation of a Jewish state?
What did Gerald Smith write about Zionism?
How is Kamal Nasser amalgamating various ideologies?

14. Nazi

What did Hitler write about Zionism?
What did von Neurath, German minister of Foreign Affairs, write that would happen once the Jewish state is established?
What did Alfred Rosenberg and Heinz Riecke write about the relationship between Zionist and Antizionist Jews?
What did Heinrich Hest write about the Jewish state?

15. Neo-Nazi

What was the medical analogy made by A.K. Chesterton?
What was John Tyndal's subtle approach on the subject of the Protocols?
What is the Zionist objective according to Martin Webster?
What is perhaps the ultimate claim advocated by the National Front?
What did Reverend Louis Farrakhan say about the 9/11 attacks and Israel?
What was the view of the British National Party on the 2014 crisis in Ukraine?

16. Holocaust Deniers

What is the foundation of Holocaust denial?
What did Paul Rassinier write about fabrication and falsification?
What did Robert Faurisson claim about "gas-chambers" and the "genocide"?
According to Arthur R. Butz, who invented the genocide and what was the proof?
What was Ditlieb Felderer's claim about Anne Frank's diary?

Christian Antizionism

17. Deicide
What is the accusation of deicide and what is the connection being made to Zionism?
What did the memorandum of the Italian Christian Association for the Defence of the Holy Places to the Italian government and the League of Nations say?
What was the view of *Christian Century*?
What was the message of Maximos V Hakim, the *Patriach of Antioch and all the Orient, of Alexandria and of Jerusalem*?

18. Non-belief
What is the rational of the non-belief of Jews in the Christian religion?
What was the position of cardinal Merry del Val, the Vatican's Secretary of State?
What was the position of Pope Pius X?
According to *Christian Century*, what should Jews do and why?
What would happen if the Jews do not implement the programme advocated by *Christian Century*?

19. Other Christian Arguments
What is the idea of Temporariness?
What is the Replacement theology?
What is the justification of Devine act in the opposition to Zionism?
Explain the use of quotes from the New Testament to justify opposition to Zionism?
Explain the interpretation of the concept of Election to justify opposition to Zionism?
What is the view of Millenerian Christians?
What is the attitude by some Christian Antizionists with regards to the use of violence?
What are Reverend Sizer's arguments against Zionism?
Why is the reliance on the ideology of the Left by Christian Antizionists paradoxical?

Jewish Antizionism

20. Emancipationism
What was the rational of Emancipationist Antizionism, both the assimilationists and those who wanted to integrate in Gentile society?
What was the view of Emancipationist Antizionists on Antisemitism?
Why did the Emancipationist Antizionists believe that Zionism was defeatist?
What did the Emancipationist Antizionists write about dual loyalty?
What did the Emancipationist Antizionists write about the culture of their respective country as oppose to Zionism?
What did the Emancipationist Antizionists think of the Jews as a nation?
What did the Emancipationist Antizionists think of Zionism as a form of nationalism?
Why did the Emancipationist Antizionists regard Zionism as a threat?
Name other arguments raised by Emancipationist Antizionists?

21. Protest Rabbis
Why was the Zionist idea for very religious Jews in contradiction with Judaism?
Who were the *Protest Rabbis* and what did they argue?

22. Protest Rabbis Followers
What is probably the single most important source of the *Protest Rabbis* followers?
What was the *Protest Rabbis* followers fundamental assertion?
What was the relevance of the "*Mitzvath Yishuv Eretz Israel*?"
What was the accusation of "*Nevieh Sheker*" levelled by the Antizionist Rabbis against the Zionists?
What similar biblical fate awaited the Zionists, according to the Antizionist Rabbis?
Explain the self-depiction by Antizionist Rabbi as saviours?

23. Breuer and Agudath Israel

What was the core of Breuer's objection to Zionism and Israel?
How has *Agudath Israel's* attitude to Zionism and Israel evolved over time?

24. Neturei Karta

What is the *Neturei Karta* sect?
What is the *Neturei Karta's* ideology?
What have been the activities of the American and London branches of *Neturei Karta*?

Arab and Muslim Antizionism

What is Arab and Muslim Antizionist ideology?
Who is the main driving force of Arab/Muslim Antizionism?

25. Aims

What is the aim of Arab/Muslim Antizionism?
Through what means are the aims of Arab/Muslim Antizionism expressed?
What is the difference between direct and indirect language in Arab/Muslim Antizionism?
What was Gamal Abdel Nasser Hussein's aim?
How did Al-Hourani see the future?
What was the goal of Tawfiq Abdallah?
What was the plan of Ali Akbar Hashemi Rafsanjani, for the future of the state of Israel?
What does Article 22 of the 1988 Hamas Charter state about the role of Jews in the history of civilisation?

26. Libels

What are some of the scurrilous libels brought by Arabs/Muslims against Zionism/Israel?
What did the 1988 Charter of Hamas say about Zionism?
What did Mahmoud Abbas write about the figure of six million Jews murdered in the Holocaust?

27. Islam
Explain the concepts of "Dar al-Islam", "Dar al-Harb" and "Jihad", in Islam?
Explain the concept of *"Dhimmis"* in Islam?
Can you give some the examples of Arab/Muslim attitudes to Zionism/Israel laced with Islamic themes?

28. Imperialism/Colonialism
Explain the argument by Arab/Muslim Antizionists that Zionism/Israel is a colonialist/imperialist implant?
Explain how historical events are presented to justify the narrative that Israel is the advance base for imperialism?
Can you give some examples of Arab/Muslim attitudes to Zionism/Israel where the accusation of imperialism/colonialism is levelled?

29. Apartheid and Boycott, Disinvestment, Sanctions (BDS)
Explain the nature of the charge of apartheid with regards to Israel?
Explain the campaign of Boycott, Disinvestment and Sanctions?
Can you give some examples of the accusation of apartheid against Israel and the epousal of the campaign of BDS by Arab/Muslims?

30. Coalescences of Antizionist Ideologies
What is the coalescences of Antizionist ideologies?
Can you give three different ways to show the coalescences of Antizionist ideologies?
Explain the use of a common denominator by different Antizionist ideologies as a means to achieve their goal?
Explain the act of borrowing ideological elements from each other as a feature of different Antizionist ideologies?
Explain the fact that different Antizionist ideologies have operated together?

Part 3: Is Antizionism Antisemitic? Other Dimensions

31. Violent Antzionism
Explain the concept of Antizionism as violence?

Can you give examples of Antizionism as violence?

32. The Antisemitic Aspect of Boycotts
Explain the Antisemitic aspect of Boycotts?
Can you give examples of the Antisemitic aspect of Boycotts?

33. Acknowledgement by Antizionists of Antisemitism
Explain the concept of acknowledgement by Antizionists of Antisemitism?
Can you give examples of acknowledgements by Antizionists of Antisemitism?

34. Antizionism as Codeword
Explain the concept of Antizionism as a codeword?
Can you give examples of Antizionism as a codeword?

35. Antizionism as Double-Standard
Explain the concept of Antizionism as double-standard?
Can you give examples of Antizionism as a double-standard?

36. The Consequences of Antizionism
Explain the concept of Antisemitism as a consequence of Antizionism?
Can you give one example of Antisemitism as a consequence of Antizionism?

37. Fellow Antizionist Travellers
Explain the concept or Fellow Antizionist Travellers?
Can you give examples of Fellow Antizionist Travellers?

38. Separate Antisemitic and Antizionist Views in same individuals
Explain the concept of Separate Antisemitic and Antizionist Views in same individuals?
Can you give an example of Separate Antisemitic and Antizionist view in same individual?

39. Unintentional Antisemitism in Antizionism

Explain the concept of Unintentional Antisemitism in Antizionism?
Can you give an example of Unintentional Antisemitism in Antizionism?

Part 4: The Means of Antizionism

40. Violence

What are the violent tactics used by Antizionists?
What is known in terms of the casualties of Antizionist violence?

41. Cartoons

Can you give examples of Antizionist cartoons?

42. Boycott, Disinvestment and Sanction (BDS)

How was BDS initiated?
How has BDS developed?

43. Omissions of Facts and Misrepresentation

Why is the call for the "*Right of Return*" a case of omissions of fact and misrepresentation?
Why is the claim that Israel's treatment of Arab Israeli citizens within Israel's pre-1967 border is similar to the treatment of blacks in apartheid South Africa, a case of omissions of fact and misrepresentation?
Why is the accusation of colonialism and imperialism levelled at Zionism/Israel, a case of omissions of fact and misrepresentation?

44. Falsifications

Can you give two examples of enemies of Zionism/Israel deliberately doctor facts in order to put the country in a bad or worse light?

45. Decontextualization

Can you give an example of a failure of Antizionists to see or refuse to consider external events that explain why Israel has acted or not acted in a certain way?

46. Exaggerations
Can you give an example of when facts are being represented by Antizionists considerably worse than the way they really occurred?

47. Double Standards
Can you give an example when Zionism/Israel are judged by Antizionists according to one measure whilst the Arab countries and other parties are judged according to another measure?

48. The Spheres
What are the main areas where the campaign against Zionism and Israel have been most active?

Describe the UK campaign by Labour Unions against Zionism/Israel?

51.

Training Exercise

Readers can try to relate the following quotes to issues raised in this handbook.

1. "As a journalist I have walked through the killing fields of Iraq, Afghanistan, Lebanon and Sri Lanka and seen death close up. As a journalist I have walked through the carnage and destruction caused by acts of terrorism in Ireland, Lockerbie, London and New York. As a journalist I have walked through areas of natural disasters caused by the earthquakes of Pakistan and Kashmir and have witnessed the aftermath of the Tsunami. As a journalist I have walked through famine areas and held starving African children in my arms as they've struggled for life. But nothing, absolutely nothing prepared me for what I witnessed as one of the first journalists to enter the Jenin refugee camp after the 2002 siege. It will haunt me for the rest of my life and in my darkest moments I still cry when I think of man's inhumanity to man in that place.

   I have never before witnessed one group of people deriving so much pleasure and joy for inflicting so much pain and suffering on another group of people including their babies and infants. The injustice that is Palestine is there for all to see if only you will look". [281]

2. "Our conflict today between us and Israel is the conflict between spirit and body. Israel's global media has expanded, and

---

[281] Yvonne Ridley, British Journalist and author, http://www.foa.org.uk/publication/the-palestinian-nakba-1948-2008-60-years-of-catastrophe/, p.4, checked on 10 May 2017.

its war against the Arabs and Muslims is through sex mania which it distributes globally. Israel had to use this sex mania, as we mentioned in a previous lesson, in order to destroy the spirit of Arabs and Muslims. Everything among the Muslims has died, except for their lust. Therefore we see filth and immodesty on many satellite channels, pictures and ads for penis enlargement and for all sorts of things. All of these are contrary to modesty. Why? Because the Jews, as it is said in the Quran, believe only in the body, not in the spirit. The Jews, according to our religion, believe only in the body... What has Israel given to the world in our times, aside from moral corruption and corrupt values, aside from the use of drugs and pills? I said in a previous lesson that the CIA has a unit called the Unit for Creating the Global Mood. They look at a map: "What is appropriate for Gaza, or Jordan, or Syria? Tramadol pills (i.e., pain killers)? Mood enhancers? Hallucinatory substances?" They are produced in India, sent to Israel, and distributed in Sinai. Afterwards they are spread in the region, in order to destroy what remains of our children's values."[282]

3   Israel should set up an inquiry to disprove allegations that its medical teams in Haiti "harvested" organs of earthquake victims for use in transplants".[283]

4. Israel "undermines the international community's reaction to global warming." ... The Middle East conflict distracts the world from the real problem: man-made climate change. If extreme weather will lead to the "end of the human race," as it could, add this to the list of the crimes of Israel.[284]

282 Imad Hamato, Professor of Quranic Studies at the University of Palestine (in Gaza), Official PA TV, *This is Our Religion*, June 12, 2015, https://www.palwatch.org/main.aspx?fi=1100&doc_id=17259, checked on 10 May 2017. See also video clip, http://www.palwatch.org/main.aspx?fi=767&-fld_id=767&doc_id=20874, checked on 10 May 2017.
283 Baroness Tonge, Liberal member of British House of Lords, https://www.thejc.com/news/uk-news/tonge-investigate-idf-stealing-organs-in-haiti-1.13971, checked on 10 May 2017.
284 Clare Short, a member of the British Parliament and past Secretary for

5. "You need to understand the Israeli occupation in order to understand how I can legitimise the means of the Palestinian resistance. It is a long term colonial, racist settling occupation. It is an uprooting occupation. The consequences of the Zionist ideology [Israel for Jews only] is that Palestinians are killed every day, that young people are disabled in large numbers by Israeli bullets, that people are arrested, that moving freely becomes impossible…Killing yourself and others for a cause has been practised by all nations and at all times….We should look to the circumstances, which lead people to do it. It is not solely an Islamic phenomenon….They are desperate and cannot find another way of resistance. They are fighting for a cause, and they have nothing to loose. We as Palestinians need something to loose in order to make this stop. People are not killing themselves for fun, and Islamic justification can only be found in very harsh circumstances. I am not justifying it. I just try to explain the motives, and how to stop it." [285]

6. "[T]oday the Gaza Strip cannot anymore [be] considered just as an open air prison. It has become a concentration camp whose occupants are victims of the crimes committed by their jailers…"[286]

International Development, *The Wall Street Journal,* https://www.wsj.com/articles/SB118877270728215947, 3 September 2007, checked on 11 May 2017.

285 Interview with Rifat Kassis, Executive Director of the East Jerusalem YMCA from *"Deliver us from Occupation: Report from the International YMCA-YWCA Observer in Palestine: No. 13,"* 30 August 2001, *World Alliances of YMCAs, Special Consultative Status with United Nations Economic and Social Council,* accredited by the *UN Committee on the Exercise of the Inalienable Rights of the Palestinian People,* http://www.humanrightsvoices.org/victims/ngos/un_ngo_connection/reports/?c=3&zoom_highlightsub=publications, checked on 11 May 2017.

286 Excerpt from *"Oral statement by the American Association of Jurists to the UN Human Rights Council, Agenda Item 7, March 23, 2015," American Association of Jurists,* Accredited with Special Consultative Status by United Nations Economic and Social Council, http://www.humanrightsvoices.org/assets/images/panels/list_10/Report-on-UN-NGOs-Spreading-Antisemitism-Terror-September-2016.pdf, checked on 11 May 2017.

7. "Typical expulsion pattern of a Palestinian village followed these lines:…They were kept in crammed concentration camps…[V]ictims are entitled to compensation in the same way as Jewish victims are now paid compensation of billions of dollars for their suffering in Nazi slave labour camps."[287]

8. "…[T]here are certainly some aspects of Israel's policy toward the Palestinians that bear a clear resemblance to the Nazis' oppression…"Genocide" -- defined by the UN Convention as the intention "to destroy, in whole or in part, a national, ethnical, racial, or religious group" -- most aptly describes Israel's efforts, akin to the Nazis', to erase an entire people.… Israel most likely does not care about how systematic its efforts at erasure are, or how rapidly they proceed, and in these ways it differs from the Nazis. There are no gas chambers; there is no overriding urgency. Gas chambers are not needed… little girls riddled with bullets here, infants beheaded by shell fire there; a little massacre here, a little starvation there… dispossession is the name of the game… [T]he people will die, the nation will die without a single gas chamber. Or so the Israelis hope…Israel has given itself the right to erase the Palestinian presence in Palestine -- in other words, to commit genocide by destroying "in whole or in part, a national, ethnical, racial, or religious group."…[G]ross injustice such as the Nazis and Israel have inflicted on innocent people cannot prevail for long." [288]

---

[287] Excerpt from *"Palestinian Forced Labour Camps,"* Near East Cultural and Educational Foundation of Canada, Accredited by the UN *Committee on the Exercise of the Inalienable Rights of the Palestinian People,* http://www.humanrightsvoices.org/assets/images/panels/list_10/Report-on-UN-NGOs-Spreading-Antisemitism-Terror-September-2016.pdf, checked on 11 May 2017.

[288] Excerpt from *"Does It Matter What You Call It? Genocide or Erasure of Palestinians,"* Women for Palestine - Australians for Palestine, Accredited by *the Committee on the Exercise of the Inalienable Rights of the Palestinian People,* http://www.humanrightsvoices.org/assets/images/panels/list_10/Report-on-UN-NGOs-Spreading-Antisemitism-Terror-September-2016.pdf, checked on 11 May 2017.

9 "Jews in Europe and around the world are complaining that what is called anti-Semitic feelings are growing in the different countries and are expressed in an openly violent manner. This is, of course, in reaction to the barbaric war Israel is fighting against the civilian population in Gaza and Palestine. Not only in Germany, where one is especially sensitive to this kind of sentiment, but also in France and other European countries where there are anti-Israel demonstrations often voicing anti-Jewish sentiments such as 'all Jews should be gassed'. Jewish people residing in Europe are reportedly worried and thinking about leaving the countries where they have resided for a long time or are publicly opposing Israel's stand. How come they don't realize or nobody has explained to them that this is an understandable reaction of people who feel helpless in the face of the barbarity that Israel is committing against helpless civilians in Gaza, and nobody, neither the United Nations, the European Union nor any human-rights organizations, is able to stop this ongoing genocide. In the same way as anti-American feelings have been on the rise in the Arab and Muslim world after the mess the US has created in Iraq, Afghanistan, Libya and Syria, there is a backlash on Israel and on Jews by association. Twitter and social media are running a boycott campaign telling people not to buy any Jewish items or services related to or tainted with Jewish money. The fallout of such a campaign could outlast the Gaza war for years or even decades as some countries have started to stop importing fruits and vegetables from Israel?"[289]

---

289 Pakistani journalist Ali Ashraf Khan in English-language daily *Saudi Gazette*, 12 August 1914, https://www.memri.org/reports/article-saudi-gazette-global-rise-antisemitism-understandable-reaction-gaza-war, checked on 11 May 2017.

52.

Discussion Points

1. "Supporters of Israel label any criticism of the State of Israel as Antisemitic".

2. "Antizionism is not to be confused with Antisemitism".

3. "Arabs cannot be Antisemitic because they are a Semitic people".

4. "The atrocities of the Holocaust are used as a whitewash to cover for the abuses committed by Israel".

5. "It is legitimate to criticise the acts of any state in the world including Israel".

6. "Not every act of Boycott, Disinvestment and Sanction (BDS) is Antisemitic".

7. "The better you know your adversary, the better you are able to fight it".

8. "Accusations of Antisemitism levelled at Antizionists are used to silence them".

9. "The occasional excesses of Antizionists are an understandable reaction to the sufferings of the Palestinians".

10. "As an Antizionist, I cannot be Antisemitic because some of my best friends are Jews".

11. "Antizionism cannot be Antisemitic because there are many Jews who are Antizionists".

12. "The fight against Antizionism is only the latest instalment of the fight against the oldest form of hatred in the history of mankind".

Index

Abbas 83, 85, 91, 142
Abode of Islam 87
Abode of War 87
Abraham 49, 66, 74, 138
Acts 9, 12, 20, 21, 39, 66, 84, 98, 100, 114, 125, 147, 152
Adler 27
Against the Jews 101
Agudath Israel 8, 76-78, 142
Ahasverus 30
Algemeyner Yidisher Arbeter Bund in Lite, Poylṇ un Rusland 34
Ali 82, 105, 142
Allah 82, 88
Allah Akbar 88
Al Quds 105
Al-Soudi 85
American 45-47, 52, 58, 61, 78, 86, 93, 101, 102, 138, 142, 149, 151
American Communist Party 45, 138
Anarchists 94
Anglo-American 47
Anglo-French hegemony 32
Anti-Christ 52
Anti-Christian 57
Anti-Israel Antizionism 19, 81, 136
Anti-Socialist 35
Apartheid 8, 80, 92, 93, 112, 123, 126, 143, 145
Arab 5, 8, 12, 19, 22, 24, 28, 32, 36, 37, 45, 48, 56, 62, 80-82, 84, 85, 87, 88, 90, 92-95, 100, 101, 104, 107, 119, 125-127, 131, 135, 137, 142, 143, 145, 146, 151
Arabic East 91

Arabism 88
Arab-Israeli 5, 22, 28, 62, 119, 135
Arab-Israeli conflict 5, 22, 28, 62, 135
Arab Israelis 126
Arab Republic 104
Arabs 12, 33, 41, 45-47, 56, 78, 80, 83, 86, 100, 108, 126, 142, 148, 152
ArtMalaga 102
Aryan 47
Asia Minor 32, 155
Assimilationists 55, 141
Association of Rabbis in Germany 73
Austria 127
Autonomism 34, 137
Avineri 109
Babylonian 37
Balfour Declaration 36, 43, 90, 137
Basel 73
Basle 51
Bauberot 111
Bauer 27
BAZO 104
BDS 8, 21, 22, 80, 92-94, 101-103, 109, 123, 124, 132, 143, 145, 152
Beatitudes 66
Beethoven 71
Beirut 45, 53, 66, 67, 92, 107, 128
Belgian 49
Bernstein 7, 38, 137
Bethlehem 93
Bible 59, 65, 74
Biblical 75, 141
Bir Zeit University 91
Bismark 71
Black Hundreds 105

Board of Deputies of British Jews 71
Bolshevik 57, 111
Bolsheviks 43, 57
Bourgeoisie 38, 40, 44, 49
Boycott 8, 9, 12, 21, 22, 80, 92-94, 100-102, 110, 112, 123, 132, 135, 136, 143, 145, 151, 152
Boycott, Divestment and Sanction 21, 92, 123, 132, 136
Boycott, Divestment, Sanctions 12, 92, 110, 123
Boycott Office 100
Boycotts 8, 12, 100, 102, 103, 110, 124, 132, 135, 144
Bradford 105
Brandeis University 109
Brenner 50, 138
Breuer 8, 76, 142
Britain 36, 45, 55, 90, 98, 110, 112, 127
Britain's 43, 121
British 32, 36, 41, 46, 50, 56, 57, 67, 71, 90, 95, 101, 103, 104, 111, 113, 114, 127, 132, 137-139, 147, 148
British Antizionist Organisation 104, 132
British Mandate 90
British National Front 56
British National Party 57, 139
Brixton 114
Brooklyn 78
Brussels 98
Buenos Aires 98
Bund 7, 34-37, 39, 137
Bundism 36
Bundist 37
Bundists 34, 35, 40, 137
Butler 102
Butz 58, 59, 139
Capitalism 41, 47, 127
Cardinal Merry del Val 63, 140
Castroists 94
Catholicism 54
Central Committee of the Bund Central Committee of the Bund 34
Chesterton 56, 139
Chinese 94
Christ 52, 61, 63- 66
Christian 7, 8, 52, 53, 60, 62-67, 95, 111, 139, 140
Christian Century 61, 62, 64, 140
Christianity 60, 64, 67, 68
Christians 51, 61, 62, 66-68, 87, 126, 140
Christian Students Association 111
Church 53, 61, 63, 64, 67
Church of England 67
Civilta Cattolica 52, 139
Class-state 35
Code Word 8, 104
Cohen 71
Collusion 50
Colonialism 8, 32, 80, 90, 126, 127, 137
Comintern 54
Communism 68, 72
Communist 7, 29, 41, 45-47, 94, 138
Communists 94
Conservative Party 105
Corbyn 50, 95, 103
Cossack 105
Coulibaly 99
Council of the Arab 100
Countries 7, 12, 14, 21, 39, 40, 45, 49, 71, 85, 87, 92, 100, 107, 112, 126, 131, 132, 138, 146, 151
Cracow 35
Czar of Russia 31
Damascus 84
Dar al-Harb 87
Dar al-Islam 87, 143
David 5, 12, 35, 37, 50, 71, 104, 114
Day of Redemption 74
Decontextualization 9, 129, 145
Dehumanisation 19, 27, 136
Dehumanizing 19, 20, 81
Deicide 8, 61, 140
Delegitimatization 19

Delegitimization 19, 27, 136, 137
Delegitimizing 19, 81
Demonization 19, 136, 157
Demonizing 19, 20, 81
Der Fraind 35
Der Jud 35, 38
Dershowitz 11
Deutsch Franzosische Jahrbucher 28
Dhimmis 87, 143
Di Arbeter Shtime 34
Diaspora 14, 31, 34-36, 98, 104, 111
Die Welt 73
Differentiation 22, 136
Divestment 12, 21, 22, 80, 92, 94, 110, 123, 132, 136
Dual loyalty 71, 108, 141
Durban 123
Double-Standard 8, 107, 144
Double Standards 9, 21, 131, 146
Egypt 32, 81, 83, 84, 90, 93
EgyptAir 83
Elie Kedourie 12
Emancipationist 69, 70, 141
Emancipationism 8, 70, 141
Emancipationists 71
Engels 27
Enlightenment 70
EU 67, 111
Euphrates 85
European 29, 71, 91, 112, 151
Europe 48, 51, 79, 91, 98, 112, 151
Europeans 24, 58
Facebook 105, 113, 115, 120, 122
Falsification 9, 58, 128, 139, 145
Farrakhan 86, 139
Far-right 104
Fascists 50
Fatherland 73
Faurisson 58, 139
Faust 71
Fellow traveller 111
Final Solution 121
Found a fertile terrain amongst Muslim, Arab, Christian and 95

Fourth National BDS Conference 93
France 104, 127, 151
Frank's 59, 139
Freedland 110
Freemasonry 52
French 32, 58, 104, 111
Galicia 39
Galuth 36
Gauleiters 48
Gaza 12, 82, 101, 111, 128, 129, 148, 149, 151
Gaza Strip 12, 149
Gaza War 111, 151
Geiger 72
General Assembly 78, 101, 125, 131
General Assembly of the United Nations 101
General Jewish Workers' Union in Lithuania, Poland and Russia 34
Gentile 70, 71, 141
Gentiles 37, 54
German 29, 47, 49, 54, 55, 58, 71, 73, 74, 139
Germany 21, 72, 73, 151
Germany's 54
God 28, 61, 62, 65, 66, 73, 75-77
God is Great 88
God's 61, 66, 75, 76
Gospel 65
Government 20, 31, 35, 36, 41, 47, 52, 61, 77, 92, 140
Goyim 54
Great Britain 36, 45, 55, 112, 127
Greek-Catholic 62, 67
Grenfell 105
Guardians of the City 78
G4S 93
Hamas 80, 85, 89, 129, 142
Hamouda 91
Hashmira 93
Hebrew 74, 109
Hebrew University of Jerusalem 109
Heine 30
Hersh 37

Herzl 31, 41, 63, 72, 73, 137, 138
Hest 55, 139
Hezbollah 80
Higher Arab Committee 100
Hirsh 12, 50, 103, 114
Hitler 47, 50, 54, 85, 105, 111, 139
Hitler's 48, 85
Holocaust 20, 21, 37, 51, 58, 67, 78, 83, 85, 102, 136, 139, 142, 152
Holocaust Deniers 51, 58, 67, 139
Holy Books 65, 74
Holy Land 61, 63, 65, 74
Holy Spirit 66
Holy War 87
Holy Writ 73
House of Israel 74
Human Rights Council 131, 149
Hungary 127
Hussain 105
Hussein 81, 91, 127, 142
Hyper Cacher 99
IHRA 20, 136
Imperialism 8, 32, 41, 44, 46, 47, 49, 53, 80, 87, 90, 91, 95, 126, 127, 143, 145
India 29, 148
International Affairs 16, 48
International Holocaust Remembrance Alliance 20, 21, 136
International of the Bund 36
Intersectionality 22, 136
Iran 67, 80, 95, 98
Iraq 55, 86, 147, 151
ISIS 80
Islam 8, 86-88, 143
Islamic 12, 80, 82, 85, 87, 94, 105, 127, 143, 149
Islamic Human Rights Commission 105
Islamic Republic 82
Islamic State 80
Islamist 98
Ismael 104
Israel Defence Forces 102, 112

Israel, Fait Colonial 49, 50
Israeli Embassy 101, 104
Italian 47, 61, 140
Italian Christian Association for the Defence of the Holy Places 61, 140
Italy 127
Jenin 130, 147
Jeremiah 75
Jerusalem 19, 22, 34, 48, 55, 62-64, 74, 76, 78, 99, 104, 107, 109, 140, 149
Jesus Christ 61, 64
Jesuit 52
Jesus 21, 61, 64, 65, 67
Jewish Film Festival 101
Jewish Home 43, 76
Jewish Museum 98
Jewish People 11, 20, 21, 33, 37, 40, 41, 63-67, 72, 109, 110, 151
Jewish Socialist party 34
Jihad 87, 88, 143
Jihadi 98
Jihadist 99
Jordan 81, 90, 93, 148
Jordan River 81,
Judaism without Embellishment 47, 138
Judah 37
Kaplan 112
Karl Marx 27, 28, 137
Kautsky 27, 29-33, 39
Khodre 65
Khomeini 82
Kichkos 47
Kingdom of God 65
King Solomon 55
Knights of Normalization 83
Kosher 99, 101, 114
Kreitsky 27
Kurds 126
Kuwait 127
Labour 29, 36, 50, 95, 103, 105, 121, 132, 146, 150
Labour force 36

Labour Party 50, 95, 103
Labour Unions 132, 146
Lassalle 30
Lawfare 22, 136
Lawrence 114
League 52, 61, 100, 140
League of Nations 52, 61, 140
Lebanese 128
Lebanon 12, 82, 84, 93, 127, 147
Lebanon War 12
Left 7, 27, 29, 43, 48-50, 67, 69, 90, 94, 95, 126, 137, 138, 140
Leftwing 132
Leninists 49
Lenin 7, 39, 40, 138
Leon 41, 48, 49, 61
LGBT 22, 23
LGBTQ 22
Livingstone 50
Loach 111
Lobby 67, 108, 114
London 11, 16, 28, 30, 31, 37, 38, 43, 45, 49-51, 54, 55, 63, 72, 94, 95, 101, 104, 105, 108, 110, 114, 115, 127, 142, 147
London's 78
London School of Economics 11, 16, 105, 115
London School of Economics and Political Science 11, 16
London School of Economics Student Union 105, 115
Lord 61, 64, 74, 105, 114
Lord Mancroft 101
Lord Mayor 105
LSE 105, 115
Luther 71
Machiavellian 55
Macpherson 114
Malaysian 102
Manasseh, son of Hezekiah 75
Mandate 90, 127
Maoists 49
Marcus 12, 109, 110

Marx 27, 28, 30, 38, 137
Marxism 28, 53,
Marxists 49, 94
Matisyahu 101
Matthew 66
Maximos V Hakim, the Patriach of Antioch and all the Orient, of alexandria and of Jerusalem 62
May 4, 20, 35, 37, 44-46, 52, 56, 57, 59, 62, 71, 81-83, 85, 98, 103, 109, 110, 111, 114, 115, 120-122, 147-151
Meccan 89
Medem 36
Mediterranean Sea 81
Mein Kampf 54
Merah 98
Messiah 28, 49, 74
Middle Ages 30
Middle East 12, 16, 43, 48, 53, 66, 80, 148
Middle East Media Research Institute 80
Millenarians 67
Min Hameitsar 78
Minister of Foreign Affairs 54, 139
Mitzvath Yishuv Eretz Israel 74, 141
Modus vivendi 56
Mohammed 102
Montefiore 71
Moscow 39, 54, 85
Moses 88
Moughrabi 92, 93
Movement 12, 27, 29, 31, 33, 40, 41, 43, 46, 57, 63, 70, 74, 85, 91, 102, 103, 110, 123, 124, 126, 127, 132, 135
Mozart 71
Munich 73
Muslim 8, 24, 80, 81, 87, 90, 92, 95, 126, 142, 143, 151
Muslims 80, 83, 86, 87, 143, 148
Muslim Brotherhood 80
Mussolini 47

Nasser 53, 81, 90, 139, 142
National Council of Palestinian Jewry 76
National Home 76, 90
National Socialist Germany 21
National Union of Students 101, 104
Nazi 7, 48, 54, 57, 83, 102, 139, 150
Nazis 21, 50, 51, 54, 55, 85, 110, 150
Nazism 56, 85, 105, 110, 138
Nelson 12, 100-102, 132, 135
Nemmouche 98
Neo-Nazi 7, 51, 56, 139
Neo-Nazis 51, 56
neo-cons 57
Neturei Karta 8, 78, 142
Netanyahu 86
Neurath 54, 139
Nevieh Sheker 75, 141
New Statesman 114
New Testament 65, 66, 140
New Left 29
NGO 93, 120, 123, 149
NGO Declaration 123
Nihilism 72
Nile 85
Non-Communist countries 7, 45, 138
Non-Governmental Organisations 123
"No Platform" for Racism 101
Norwich Union 101
Of Islam leader 86
Old Testament 65, 76
On the Jewish Question 28, 41, 49
Orthodox 31, 47, 67, 69, 76, 78
Orthodox Russian nation 31
Ottoman Sultan 31
Pale of Settlement 34, 40
Palestine 28, 31-35, 37, 41, 45, 49, 53-55, 62, 65-67, 70, 73, 78, 80, 81, 84, 85, 87-90, 92, 93, 100, 101, 103, 106, 107, 111, 119, 120, 122, 123, 132, 137, 138, 147-151
Palestine Authority 123
Palestine Communist Party 45, 138

Palestine Liberation Organisation 78
Palestine Media Watch 80
Palestine Solidarity Campaign 120, 132
Palestinian 12, 32, 45, 53, 54, 58, 76, 80, 81, 85, 92, 93, 98, 101, 102, 108, 112, 120, 123, 125, 127-130, 132, 135, 137, 147, 149, 150
Palestinian Authority 85, 130
Palestinian Prisoners 93
Palestinian Liberation Front 85
Palestinians 12, 22, 62, 83, 84, 93, 107, 108, 111, 149, 150, 152
Paris 28, 39, 48, 53, 57, 58, 61, 62, 65, 99, 100, 104, 105, 127
Parliament 77, 126, 148
Parties 7, 45, 88, 107, 131, 138, 146
Partition's 47
Pentagon 86
Peretz 47
Pink-washing 23, 136
Plehve 31, 137
PLO 85
Poland 34, 36
Polish 49
Politicidal Antizionism 19, 81, 136
Pope Pius X 63, 140
Pour La Palestine 53, 62, 65-67
POW's 48
Powers 43, 46, 90, 127
Prittie 100, 101
Pro-Palestinian 101, 102, 132
Protestrabbiner 73
Protestant 61
Protocols 51, 56, 83, 85, 139
Protocols of the Elders of Zion 51, 83, 85
Proudhon 27
Pro-Western 22
PSC 132
Quran 87, 89, 148
Rabbi 8, 74, 75, 78, 98, 141
Rabbis 8, 40, 73, 74, 75, 84, 105, 141
Racism 5, 22, 57, 59, 95, 101, 111,

114, 123
Rasse und Judentum 30-32
Rassinier 58, 139
Reactionary 30, 40, 44, 127, 137
Rejectionists 80
Resolution 194, 125
Reuters 92, 128, 129
Reverend 67, 86, 139, 140
Revolution 36, 43, 53, 82, 90, 111
Riecke 55, 139
Riecke's 55
Right 13, 21, 34, 56, 62, 71, 72, 75, 85, 88, 94, 105, 107, 111, 115, 120, 125, 126, 131, 150
Right of Return 125, 145
Right-wing 51, 95
Robert Wistrich 12, 94
Rodinson 49, 50
Rosenberg 55, 139
Rothschild 101
Russia 31, 34, 35, 39, 43, 44, 57
Russian 31, 35, 36, 43, 57, 67, 105, 138
Russian Minister of Interior 31
Sainsbury 101
Sassoon 102
Sanctions 12, 22, 80, 92, 110, 123, 136, 143
Scarman 114
Scherer 37, 137
Scottish Parliament's Cross Party Group on Palestine 103
Secretary General 78, 92, 131
Second International 29
Second World War 44, 48, 50, 56, 78
Secretary of State 63, 140
Shabtai Zvi 72
Sheiks 94
Shonfeld 78
Sinai war 90
Sizer 67, 95, 140
Six-Day war 12, 47, 138
Small 32, 49, 78, 80, 101, 105, 112
Smith 52, 139

Social Democracy 29
Socialism 27, 34, 38, 40, 42, 44, 127, 137
Socialist 21, 27, 30, 34, 41
Socialist Movement 27
Socialist Zionists 27
Solomon 37, 55
South Africa 92, 93, 123, 126, 145
Soviet 28, 43, 44, 47, 48, 85, 94, 105
Soviet Embassy 104, 105
Soviets 47
Soviet Union 44, 47, 85, 127, 138
Spain 101, 102
Spinoza 30, 38
Stalin 27
Stalin's 42
Stalinists 49
Stamford Hill 78
Steinberg 74, 75
Student Union 105, 115
Sudan 91
Supreme Court 126
Svirsky 104
Swedish 59
Synagogue 57
Synagogues 105
Syria 84, 98, 127, 148, 151
Talmud 55, 59, 84
Tel Aviv 43, 58
Terre Promise, Trop Promise- Genese du Conflict Israelo- Palestinien (1882-1948) 100
The Economic War 100, 101
The Guardian 16, 110, 129
The Holocaust Victims Accuse 78
The Nation 86, 114, 150
The Palestinian Civil Society Calls for Boycott, Divestment and sanctions [BDS] Against Israel 123
The Protocols of the Elders of Zion 51, 83, 85
Theological Commission 67
The Times 16, 71, 108, 113
Third World 94

161

Torah 76, 77, 88
Tory Party 106
Toulouse 98
Trade unions 124, 132
Trades Union Congress 132
Tricycle Theatre 101
Trostky 42
Trotskyist 29, 49
Trotskyists 49, 94
Trotskysts 50
Tsarist government 35
Twin Towers 86
TUC 132
Tyndall 56, 57
UCU 132
Uddin 105, 115
UK 5, 16, 71, 101, 132, 146
Ukraine 57, 139
Ukrainian Academy of Science 47
Ukranian 57
Ukrainian 47
UN 92, 101, 120, 125, 127, 131, 149, 150
UN Charter 131
Union 34, 44, 47, 85, 101, 104, 105, 114, 115, 124, 127, 132, 138, 151
United 12, 13, 36, 37, 46, 52, 53, 78, 92, 101, 104, 123, 125, 131, 149, 151
United Command of the Palestinian Revolution 53
UN Economic and Social Commission of Western Asia 92
United Kingdom 13
United Nations 12, 52, 78, 92, 101, 123, 125, 131, 149, 151
United Nations Secretary-General 78
United States 36, 37, 46, 52
University Lecturers Union 132
Upper Egypt 83
US 67, 151
U.S. 83, 90, 91, 108
USA 90
Va'ad Leoumi 76
Valencia 101

Vatican's 63, 140
Vatican State 54
Vicar 67
Vilna 34
Walker 113
Wandering Jew 30
Warburg 101
Warsaw 58, 74
Webster 56, 57, 139
Weinstock 28, 49, 100, 127
Weissmandel 78
West 12, 29, 70, 80, 90, 91, 93, 94, 127
Western 22, 23, 39, 40, 47, 49, 53, 90-92
West Bank 12, 90, 93, 127
West Bank of Jordan 90
Wilby 114
Wistrich 12, 28, 29, 38, 41-43, 94
Workers 34-36, 43, 45, 46
World Centre of contemporary Jewish documentation 58
World Danger 55
World Conference against Racism, Racial Discrimination, Xenophobia and Related Intolerance 123
World Conference of Christians for Palestine 66, 67
World Socialism 38, 42
World War II 21, 59
Yom Kippur 84
Zio 105, 115
Zionist Congress 51, 73
Zionist Movement 31, 46, 57, 85, 91, 124, 127
Zionist-Socialists 36